TURKEY

Violations of Free Expression in Turkey

Human Rights Watch
New York · Washington · London · Brussels

ISBN 1-56432-226-2
Library of Congress Catalog Card Number: 99-60862

Addresses for Human Rights Watch:
350 Fifth Avenue, 34th Floor, New York, NY 10118-3299
Tel: (212) 290-4700, Fax: (212) 736-1300, E-mail: hrwnyc@hrw.org

1522 K Street, NW, #910, Washington, DC 20005-1202
Tel: (202) 371-6592, Fax: (202) 371-0124, E-mail: hrwdc@hrw.org

33 Islington High Street, N1 9LH London, UK
Tel: (171) 713-1995, Fax: (171) 713-1800, E-mail: hrwatchuk@gn.apc.org

15 Rue Van Campenhout, 1000 Brussels, Belgium
Tel: (2) 732-2009, Fax: (2) 732-0471, E-mail: hrwatcheu@gn.apc.org

Web Site Address: http://www.hrw.org
Gopher Address://gopher.humanrights.org:5000/11/int/Human Rights Watch
Listserv Address: To subscribe to the list, send an e-mail message to
majordomo@igc.apc.org with "subscribe Human Rights Watch-news" in the body
of the message (leave the subject blank).

ACKNOWLEDGMENTS

This report is based primarily on research conducted by Christopher Panico, then a researcher at Human Rights Watch, in Turkey in August, September, and November 1997. It was written by Mr. Panico, and edited by Jeri Laber, senior adviser to Human Rights Watch, and Holly Cartner, executive director of the Europe and Central Asia division of Human Rights Watch. Parts were edited by Elizabeth Andersen, advocacy director, Human Rights Watch, and supplemental research was conducted by Kumru Toktamis. Invaluable production assistance was provided by Patrick Minges, publications director, and by Alexandra Perina and Joshua Sherwin, associates, Human Rights Watch.

Human Rights Watch would like to acknowledge and thank the many individuals whose contributions made this report possible.

TABLE OF CONTENTS

You can say there is no freedom of expression, you can say there is press freedom, and you are right in both statements. It's not like in a typical dictatorship—the borders are not clear, you can't know where they are. The application of the law is arbitrary. But in many ways the arbitrariness is worse. You don't know when you will get into trouble.

Ahmet Altan, novelist and political columnist

Something that occurred in 1985 is indicative of free expression, as well as the general level of democracy in Turkey. Emil Galip was meeting with someone from a foreign human rights organization and showed her a book outlining violations of human rights that had just been published here. The visitor lamented the abuses, but commented that things were not that bad if you could publish a book about them. Emil Bey called me later and was worried that he gave the wrong impression. But that is the situation here.

Erbil Tüşalp, political columnist, *Radikal*

I. SUMMARY

This report examines the state of free expression in Turkey. It focuses largely on the print and broadcast media, and to a lesser extent on freedom of speech in politics. The report deals with the period from 1995 to the present; when necessary, however, earlier periods are also explored. Given the plethora and ideological breadth of the media and of political parties in Turkey, this study cannot hope to deal with each and every newspaper, author, or political group. Rather, it uses representative cases to highlight violations of the internationally-protected right to free expression.

The press in Turkey—in the vernacular of psychiatry—suffers from multiple personality disorder. When reporting on the vast majority of issues, such as domestic party politics or the economy, the media today is lively and unrestricted—indeed often sensational. Nearly all points of view are expressed, from radical Islamist to Kurdish-nationalist and dyed-in-the-wool Kemalist. The boundaries of criticism are nearly limitless when reporting on most issues.

Such freedom, however, ends at the border of a number of sensitive topics. Alongside the arena of free discussion there is a danger zone where many who criticize accepted state policy face possible state persecution. Risky areas include the role of Islam in politics and society, Turkey's ethnic Kurdish minority and the conflict in southeastern Turkey, the nature of the state, and the proper role of the military.

Repression for reporting or writing on such topics includes the killing of journalists by shadowy death squads believed linked to or tolerated by security forces, imprisonment and fines against journalists, writers, and publishers, the closing of newspapers and journals, the banning of books and publications, denial of press access to the conflict in southeastern Turkey, the banning of political parties, and the prohibition on the use of Kurdish in broadcasting and education. Media owners and editors sometimes serve as ideological overseers, forcing journalists to practice self-censorship and, at times, firing obstreperous reporters and columnists. In addition, since mid-1997, the powerful military has started to pressure newspaper owners and editors to support its anti-fundamentalist campaign.

For its part, the Workers Party of Kurdistan (PKK), which has been waging an insurgency in southeastern Turkey for the past fourteen years, has exerted a deleterious influence on the press and press freedom. It has kidnapped and killed journalists, instituted bans against press operations in southeastern Turkey that forced most papers temporarily to close their Diyarbakır bureaus, and pressured journalists working at Kurdish-nationalist papers to practice self-censorship.

1

Even when writing on sensitive topics, however, a wide latitude holds sway, and different realities exist for different individuals. Recent films, such as Reis Çelik's *Let there be Light (Işıklar Sönmezsin)*, a frank account of the conflict in southeastern Turkey, or the depiction of police torture in Mustafa Altıoklar's *Heavy Novel (Ağır Roman)*, have pushed barriers.

Well-known columnists at mainstream papers can—and for the most part do—write critically on such topics, usually with little fear of prosecution. The introduction of private broadcasting in the early 1990s has also expanded the range of debate and discussion.

Journalists working at a Kurdish-nationalist publication, however, face likely punishment or worse for similar boldness. In 1997, for example, three journalists—two from the now defunct Kurdish nationalist *Demokrasi* paper and a reporter for the mainstream private television channel *ATV*—were arrested for interviewing two former PKK members. The state prosecutor charged that the trio of reporters had pressured the men to make their statements, which were deemed detrimental to state interests. The pair, however, had earlier given similar accounts without incident to other newspapers and to two popular television news programs. They even testified before a commission of the parliament of Turkey. The three journalists were later acquitted.

Timing also plays a role. During periods of liberalization, the doors of expression swing open, and repressive press laws, while still on the books, are often ignored by state prosecutors. During periods of crisis, on the other hand, such as an escalation in the conflict in southeastern Turkey, those very same doors are slammed shut, and state authorities invoke the full measure of the law, including against well-known journalists and writers. Oral Çalışlar, a columnist for the daily *Cumhuriyet*, interviewed the PKK leader, Abdullah Öcalan, and the head of the Socialist Party of Kurdistan, Kemal Burkay, in early 1993. His interview ran as full-page articles without incident for eighteen days. When the interviews were published in book form in September 1993, however, the State Security Court of Istanbul banned the publication and charged Mr. Çalışlar and his publisher with "separatist propaganda" under Article 8 of the Anti-Terror Law. The interview appeared in *Cumhuriyet* during an unofficial cease-fire, while the book came out during an escalation of the conflict in the fall of 1993.

Repressive actions are facilitated by Turkey's antiquated legal system and restrictive constitution, which reflect the country's more authoritarian past. The present constitution was introduced in 1982 by military authorities after the coup of 1980. It replaced the liberal constitution of 1961 which, ironically, was adopted after the coup of 1960. The penal code, while amended many times, was adopted in 1926 and is based on the Italian penal code of 1889. Some of the amendments, however, actually increased penalties.

The legal system and the constitution are negatively influenced on two concepts: an omnipotent state and the ideology of Kemalism, introduced by Mustafa Kemal, the founder of the modern Turkish state. While some may indeed argue that such concepts were necessary seventy-five years ago when the Republic of Turkey was founded and certainly were not unique to Turkey, they have little place in a world that prizes the individual and seeks to make government transparent to its citizens.

The notion of an all-powerful state, which appears to exist as a goal in and of itself, is sown throughout the 1982 constitution. Until amended in 1995, the preamble of the constitution even spoke of a "sacred state." Such concepts are also found in Turkey's legal framework. The penal code, for example, grants corporate state bodies, such as the judiciary or the army, "moral identities" that can be "insulted." Aptly titled, State Security Courts *(Devlet Güvenlik Mahkemesi)* exist to protect the state. In an effort to protect the inner workings of the state from prying eyes, civil servants are forbidden by law from speaking to the press.

The legacy of "Kemalism"—the attempt to build a homogeneous, modern society based on secular, Westernizing principles and a monoethnic Turkish identity—is manifested in the law either through vague warnings or, conversely, through absolute prohibitions. The preamble of the constitution, for example, threatens that, *"No protection shall be given to thoughts or opinions* that run counter to Turkish national interests, the fundamental principle of the existence of the indivisibility of the Turkish state and territory, the historical and moral values of Turkishness, or the nationalism, principles, reforms, and modernism of Atatürk, and that as required by the principle of secularism there shall be absolutely no interference of sacred religious feeling in the affairs of state and politics."[1] One statute of the Political Parties Law, similarly, criminalizes the creation of "ethnic minorities" while Article 312.2 of the penal code prohibits "incit[ing] people to enmity and hatred by pointing to class, racial, religious, confessional, or regional differences."

Whether officially acknowledged or not, however, society has moved beyond many of the principles of Kemalism and the "sacred state mentality." The myth of monoethnic Turkish identity has been exposed, and Turkey's citizens are increasingly aware of their different ethnic backgrounds—whether Kurdish, Circassian, Georgian, Chechen, or Laz. Attempts to attribute dubious Turkish

---

[1] Emphasis added.

ethnic backgrounds to non-Turkish groups, such as calling Kurds "Mountain Turks," have been abandoned. Even in indictments to close political parties, prosecutors have begun to acknowledge the existence of minorities. Furthermore, some principles of Kemalism have been dropped outright, such as the belief in the state ownership of enterprises and central economic planning. In fact, since 1986, the government has been aggressively pursuing a privatization campaign. Transparency, the antidote to the "sacred state," is sought by all, whether businessmen who want to change a Banking Law that conceals the identity of insolvent financial institutions or journalists who want the right to interview civil servants.

The principle of secularism as defined by Kemalism remains the most muddied and manipulated concept of all. Since the transition to multi-party democracy in 1946, all the center-right parties have appealed to religious sentiment in campaign messages despite manifest prohibitions to the contrary. Furthermore, in 1982, the military—ostensibly the guardians of the Kemalist revolution—for the first-time introduced constitutionally-mandated religious instruction in elementary and secondary schools.

The legal framework still lags far behind developments in society. Recognizing this, successive governments since 1990 have sought to liberalize laws that are used to punish free expression—without, however, addressing the underlying rationales for creating such legislation in the first place. Subsequent results have been palliative, at best. In 1991, the government repealed a law passed in 1983 that prohibited the use of Kurdish (Law No. 2932) together with Articles 141,142, and 163 of the penal code that penalized, respectively, writers found guilty of communist, Kurdish-nationalist, and Islamist activities. In place of these laws, however, the government passed the Anti-Terror Law. Articles 7 and 8 of that law are often used to punish free expression dealing with the Kurdish question. Furthermore, laws still exist that prevent broadcasting in Kurdish, teaching Kurdish in private or state schools, and using Kurdish in political campaigns. In 1995, the government was forced to amend Article 8 to narrow its scope, resulting in the releases of scores of writers and others from jail. In August 1997, the government of then Prime Minister Mesut Yılmaz suspended the sentences of a number of so-called responsible editors who had been imprisoned on free expression charges. Despite these improvements, individuals are still being charged and imprisoned on free expression charges.

Every state has a duty—indeed an obligation—to maintain public order, and Turkey faces legitimate security threats. But that responsibility must be seriously weighed against the right of the individual to express his opinions and to argue for change peacefully within a democratic system.

II. RECOMMENDATIONS

To the government of Turkey:
- investigate all "actor unknown murders" including those of journalists listed in this report;

- establish a commission consisting of the undersecretary of the Ministry of Justice, the state minister responsible for human rights, the head of the Press Council of Turkey, and a representative from the human rights community of Turkey to review sentences imposed under Articles 168 and 169 of the penal code (membership in an armed group and aiding an armed group) to those working at newspapers and other publications in order to determine whether their convictions were based on concrete evidence, and not on the mere fact of working at such a publication or the exercise of other internationally protected rights;

- repeal or amend all laws and decrees that violate international standards, including but not limited to the following:

Constitution
- repeal paragraph 5 of the preamble of the constitution, which states that,

  No protection shall be given to thoughts or opinions that run counter to Turkish national interests, the fundamental principle of the existence of the indivisibility of the Turkish state and territory, the historical and moral values of Turkishness, or the nationalism, principles, reforms, and modernism of Atatürk, and that as required by the principle of secularism there shall be absolutely no interference of sacred religious feeling in the affairs of state and politics.

- repeal Article 26.2 and Article 26.3 of the constitution, which place severe restrictions on Article 26.1, "Freedom of Expression and the Dissemination of Thought;"

- amend Articles 28.5 and 28.7 of the constitution and additional Article 1 of the Press Law to remove from prosecutors and others the right to confiscate publications without first obtaining a court order;

- repeal Article 28.10 of the constitution and additional Article 2 of the Press Law that allow courts to close publications;

- repeal Article 28.2 of the constitution, that prohibits publication in languages "prohibited by law;"

- repeal Article 42.9 of the constitution and Article 2 of the Foreign Language and Teaching Law, both of which state that, "The mother tongue of Turkish Citizens cannot be taught in any language other than Turkish;"

The Penal Code
- repeal Article 155 of the penal code, which penalizes publishing articles that "make people unwilling to serve in the military;"

- repeal Article 158 of the penal code, which prohibits "insult[ing] the President of the Republic;"

- repeal Article 159 of the penal code, which criminalizes "insulting the moral personality of Turkishness, the Republic, the Parliament, the Government, State Ministers, the military or security forces, or the Judiciary;"

- amend Articles 311 and 312.2 of the penal code, "publicly inciting a crime" and "inciting people to enmity and hatred by pointing to class, racial, religious, confessional, or religious difference" to prevent the punishment of thought;

- repeal Article 312.1 of the penal code, which prohibits "praising an action considered criminal;"

Other laws
- strip military courts of the right to try civilians for violations of the military penal code;

- repeal Article 8 of the Anti-Terror Law, which prohibits so-called "separatist propaganda;"

- repeal Article 4 of the Law Concerning the Founding and Broadcasts of Television and Radio (RTÜK) to allow broadcasting in any and all languages, and to remove vague and general broadcasting prohibitions that contradict international standards;

- amend The Law Concerning Crimes Committed Against Atatürk to limit criminal activity solely to acts contained in Article 2 of the law, which penalizes destroying, defacing, breaking, or ruining a statue, bust, or monument representing Atatürk or the grave of Atatürk. Such activities would be considered destruction of public property, punishable under international law;

- repeal Article 16 of the Press Law, which assigns a "responsible editor" to publications and articles in order to broaden criminal liability;

- repeal Article 58 of the Law Concerning Fundamental Provisions on Elections and Voter Registries to allow the use of any and all languages during political campaigns;

- repeal Article 81 of the Political Parties Law, "Preventing the Creation of Minorities;"

- repeal Article 8 of the Police Duty and Responsibility Law, which gives police the administrative right to close down plays, films, or lectures; and

- repeal Article 15 of the State Civil Servants Law, which prohibits civil servants from speaking to the press.

To the U.S. government:
- use its special relationship with the government of Turkey to encourage Turkey to adopt policies with respect to freedom of expression that comport with international standards;

- work with the Turkish government and military to live up to their commitments to improve human rights practices, including through the decriminalization of freedom of expression, a condition set by the United States State Department for the potential sale of U.S.-manufactured military helicopters to Turkey; and

- continue to promote civil society and freedom of expression in Turkey through assistance to independent Turkish non-governmental organizations.

To the Organization for Security and Cooperation in Europe:
- identify improvements in freedom of expression as an important goal to be met in advance of Turkey's hosting of the 1999 OSCE summit;

- work through the OSCE Representative on Freedom of the Media to address the legal and structural obstacles to freedom of expression in Turkey; and

- work through the OSCE High Commissioner on National Minorities to address restrictions on freedom of expression, in particular language and education rights, that relate to ethnic minorities in Turkey.

To the European Union:
- raise concerns relating to restrictions on freedom of expression with Turkish government counterparts; and

- continue to promote civil society and freedom of expression in Turkey through assistance to independent, nongovernmental organizations in Turkey.

To the Council of Europe:
- address Turkey's record on freedom of expression using the monitoring procedures of the Committee of Ministers and the Parliamentary

Assembly, calling for the legal reforms identified as necessary in this report; and

- through the Council's program of intergovernmental cooperation and assistance, provide Turkey with expert advice regarding needed reform of its laws on freedom of expression.

III. BACKGROUND

Since the beginning of the 1990s, two issues have dominated Turkey's political agenda: the place of a substantial ethnic Kurdish minority, estimated at between 10-20 percent of the population, and the proper role of Islam in an overwhelmingly Muslim though officially secular country.

Since 1984, southeastern Turkey has been the scene of serious fighting between government security forces and the PKK (Workers' Party of Kurdistan, "Partia Karkaren Kurdistan"), a militant armed Kurdish group whose explicit claims range from complete independence to regional autonomy within Turkey. The conflict, which reached a peak between 1992-1995, has been characterized by severe human rights abuses by both the security forces and the PKK. The government intensified a counterinsurgency campaign against the PKK, forcibly evacuating and burning rural villages. The majority of the more than 2,500 villages and hamlets depopulated in the region since 1984 are believed to be the result of this campaign. In 1991, an Anti-Terror Law was passed which, among other things, resulted in the repression of non-violent expression—especially concerning debate on the Kurdish issue—and the imprisonment of writers and intellectuals. By 1992, the conflict in the southeast entered a new spiral. Torture and deaths in detention increased, as did disappearances under mysterious circumstances. A wave of so-called "actor unknown murders" believed linked to or tolerated by security forces struck Kurdish nationalist intellectuals and journalists and also suspected PKK members, with the number of such deaths rising to 1,288 between 1992 and 1995.

For its part, the PKK is also guilty of severe human rights abuses, intimidating and murdering those who stand in its way. The PKK assassinated individuals suspected of "cooperating with the state," such as teachers, civil servants, and former PKK members. Between 1992-1995, the PKK is believed to have committed at least 768 politically-motivated assassinations. In addition, it launched attacks against villages that had joined the government civil-defense "village guard" program, killing village guards and their families alike in large-scale massacres.

There were some attempts, not entirely unsuccessful, to adopt a more liberal policy regarding ethnic Kurds. In 1991, Mr. Turgat Özal, the president, succeeded in abolishing Law. No. 2932 forbidding the use of Kurdish and also broke down the taboo about discussing the Kurdish issue in public debate. That effort, combined with the introduction of private television, spawned a raucous and largely unlimited debate on the Kurdish question that lasted through 1993. In November 1991, Mr. Suleyman Demirel, now president and then the newly-elected prime minister from the center-right True Path Party (DYP), spoke about acknowledging the "Kurdish reality." Although Turkey softened the Anti-Terror Law in 1995 and eased some restrictive articles of the constitution the same year, further attempts at liberalization regarding the Kurdish question fell victim to the escalating violence described above. In September 1995, the coalition government between the DYP and the center-left Republican People's Party (CHP), which had been in power since the October 1991 parliamentary elections, collapsed. New elections were held in December 1995. To the shock of many, the Islamist Welfare Party (RP) received a thin plurality with 21.4 percent of the vote.[2] After the short-lived failure of an interim government, the Welfare Party formed a coalition government with the center-right DYP in July 1996.

The Welfare Party's leader, Mr. Necmettin Erbakan, who had served as Deputy Prime Minister in three earlier coalition governments in the 1970s, became prime minister. The Erbakan government quickly abandoned the hazily-defined, purportedly Islam-based "Just Order" reform program on which it had campaigned. Nevertheless, it infuriated the powerful military and other sectors of the secular establishment through its attempt to legalize certain aspects of Islam at odds with Turkey's constitution, such as allowing female civil servants to wear head scarves, and by its efforts to improve ties with states such as Libya and Iran. The military establishment, further upset by the Welfare Party's attempt to pack the bureaucracy with its supporters and of intemperate statements by some party leaders, declared "fundamentalism" Turkey's number one threat. In February 1997, the military dominated National Security Council (MGK) presented Mr. Erbakan with an eighteen-point program to rein in Islamist activity, including closing the first form of state supported "İmam-Hatip" religious schools. The government promised to implement the program, but did little. On June 11, 1997, the General Staff headquarters issued a statement threatening that "weapons would be used if necessary in the struggle against fundamentalism." One week later, Mr. Erbakan resigned. In February 1998, after a trial in the Constitutional Court, the Welfare Party was closed and several of its leaders, including Mr. Erbakan, were barred from politics for five years.[3]

---

[2]In 1991, in an election alliance with another party, the Welfare Party received 16.4 percent of the vote; in 1987, running alone, it garnered around 7 percent. In 1977, the previous election it contested before 1987, its predecessor, the National Salvation Party (MSP), received around 8.3 percent of the vote.

[3]The Welfare Party reconstituted itself as the Virtue Party (Fazilet), the largest party in parliament.

Following the resignation of Mr. Erbakan, a weak coalition government was formed by Mesut Yılmaz, leader of the center-right Motherland Party, in July 1997. Mr Yılmaz in turn lost a vote of confidence in December 1998, and was replaced as Prime Minister by Bülent Ecevit, head of a small center-left party.[4] The conflict in southeastern Turkey continues, although at a much reduced level from its 1992-1995 peak. The military still considers "fundamentalism" Turkey's number one threat and has pressured the government on several occassions to take a harder line against political Islam. Early elections are scheduled for April 1999.

The military's intense reaction to political Islam must be understood as a legacy of Kemalism, the loose set of modernizing principles based on a homogenous, monoethnic Turkish identity and secular Westernization that is still recognized as Turkey's official creed. The constitution declares that it is guided by "...the concept of nationalism set forth by the Founder of the Republic of Turkey, the eternal leader and unrivaled hero Atatürk, and by the revolution and fundamental principles introduced by him...."[5] The so-called "Six Arrows of Kemalism" were adopted as the official state ideology in 1931 and made part of the constitution in 1937. They have been adopted in some form in all subsequent constitutions. The "Six Arrows" included fealty to the following principles: republicanism; secularism; nationalism; populism; statism, and reformism.[6] In its harshest application of the 1930s and 1940s, Kemalism brooked no difference or dissent, whether based on ethnicity, social class, or religion: "total cohesion and unity among all the groups who made up the people [was required] and there was no room for a conflict of interest among them."[7]

---

[4]The other two partners include the center-left Democratic Left Party (DSP) of Mr. Bülent Ecevit and the splinter Democratic Turkey Party (DTP) of Mr. Hüsammettin Cindoruk.

[5]Unofficial preamble translation.

Article 2 of the constitution pronounces Turkey, a "democratic, secular, and social state governed by the rule of law....loyal to the nationalism of Atatürk...", while Article 4 declares that Article 2 "cannot be amended nor can its amendment be put forward." Article 4 also prohibits amending or suggesting the amendment of Article 1 ("The Form of the State") and Article 3 ("The Characteristics of the Republic").

[6]The term İnkılapçılık has been translated both as "reformism" and "revolutionism." Erich J. Zürcher, *Turkey: A Modern History* (London: I.B. Tauris, 1993), pp. 189-90. Statism referred to state ownership of major industries.

[7]Feroz Ahmad, *The Making of Modern Turkey* (London: Routledge, 1993), p. 79. This concept is still held by many. Dr. Turgay Yücel, an advisor with the Justice Ministry, told Human Rights Watch that, "Turkish people don't have classes. This is the thing that our Western friends miss." Interview, Ankara, September 1997.

The principles of Kemalism as reflected in society, however, have been in flux for quite some time, at least since the adoption of multi-party democracy in 1946. Kemalism means different things to different people, and its interpretation can be manipulated for political necessity or altered to reflect changing conditions. Furthermore, the situation is complicated by the fact that Kemalism was never codified into a rigid set of rules.[8]

Religion remains one of the most contested areas. While the secular identity of Turkey, i.e. a non-Sharia state ruled by civil law, has never been seriously contested by the vast majority of the population, the exact definition of "secularism" is hotly debated. Despite strict prohibitions, nearly all the center-right parties have appealed to and flirted with—and continue to do so—religious feelings and piousness. Article 87 of the Political Parties Law, however, prohibits "the exploitation of religion and things considered religiously sacred." After the 1980 coup, even the military embraced religion as a hoped for antidote against leftist "tendencies" among the youth of Turkey. Under Article 24 of the 1982 constitution, the staunchly secular military introduced mandatory religious instruction for primary and middle-school students.[9] Even the number of İmam-Hatip religious schools, which the military successfully sought to reduce with the passage of an eight-year education bill in 1997, increased from 258 to 350 during the period of military rule, which lasted from 1980 to 1983.[10]

The concept of "nationalism," which, in its most virulent form, denied the very existence of Kurds and other non-Turkish minorities, has softened and Turkish

---

[8]Zürcher, p. 189.

[9]Article 24.4 states that, "Religious and moral education and instruction will be conducted under the supervision and control of the state. Religious culture and moral instruction will be among the mandatory courses taught in primary and middle-level educational institutions...." The implementation of mandatory, Hanefi Sunni-based instruction caused consternation among Turkey's Alevi population which practice a heterodox, syncretic form of Shiism.

[10]Ahmad, p. 219.

officials now acknowledge their presence.[11] Turkey's politicians, however, have been unable or unwilling to anchor this recognition in law.

Although under increasing criticism, the idea of an omnipotent, centralized state that transcends the individual is still very much alive in Turkey.[12] The "state" is usually construed to include the bureaucracy, the military, the police, the judiciary, the courts, and the government. Before it was amended in 1995, the preamble to the 1982 constitution even spoke of a "sacred State" (*kutsal Devlet*).

Public officials and politicians regularly invoke the "state" to defend their actions or justify restrictive policies. In a recent case in Manisa in which ten teenagers were convicted of membership in an armed group based almost exclusively on testimony taken under torture, a journalist complained that,

> How was this verdict given? It was given solely by taking police assertions (*iddiaları*) as a basis. If we continue the process of taking police assertions as evidence, we are going to experience a lot more "Manisas" in this country. When we accept the state as a sacred body and put those who work for it in a special category, we will not be able to liberate ourselves from these injustices.[13]

---

[11]In September 1995, President Demirel, for example, announced that, "I consider everyone a Turk who chooses to call himself a Turk. Together with this, if an individual demands to call himself a Kurd, I consider this person a Kurd, but as a Turkish citizen, because [he is] as a part of the Turks." Reprinted in Kemal Kirişçi and Gareth Winrow, *Kürt Sorunu: Kökeni ve Gelişmi* (Istanbul: Tarih Vakfı Yurt Yayınları, April 1997), p. 217. The work originally appeared in English as *The Kurdish Question and Turkey: An Example of Trans-State Ethnic Conflict*.

For more information on nationalism and ethnic identity see, "Restrictions on the Use of the Kurdish Language."

[12]A 1995 study commissioned by the Turkish Industrialists and Businessmens' Association (TÜSIAD), for example, called for the reform of traditional Turkish state structures. The report drew the following juxtapositions between the present state of affairs and what TÜSIAD termed "an optimal state:" sacred state vs. individual-centered state; closed, secret state vs. open/transparent state; and an authoritarian state vs. a liberal state. See *TÜSIAD*, "Optimal State," (*Optimal Devlet*), Istanbul, September 1995, pp. 17 & 27.

[13]Zeliha Midilii, "Neye dayanarak bu çocukları mahkum ettiniz?" ("What were these kids convicted on?"), *Milliyet*, Istanbul (Internet edition), January 18, 1997. The case became known as the "Manisa case," the city where the ten were arrested.

Facing the loss of his parliamentary immunity for his alleged involvement in the Susurluk scandal, Mehmet Ağar, a former police official and interior minster, defended himself by stating that, "I have committed myself to the state and to the nation, not to the parliament."[14] His co-defendant, the ethnic Kurdish parliamentarian Sedat Bucak, announced that he was, "A statist to the end."[15] A policeman on trial for the murder of a suspect during interrogation asserted that, "If you convict us, you will have convicted the state."[16]

In a more general sense, the omnipotent, "sacred" state concept obstructs the free flow of information and hinders transparency. State bodies often view non-state actors as disruptive competitors. One commentator noted that, "Indeed the military and (at least until quite recently) the civilian bureaucracy have traditionally seen themselves as the guardians of the state and the protectors of public interest. Consequently, they have viewed with suspicion all particularistic interests and political parties that represented them."[17]

Armed conflict in the southeast has heightened consciousness of the state and its territorial integrity. Under international law, every state has the right to defend its territory from both foreign and domestic attack, and Turkey certainly has faced a legitimate security threat from the PKK. States do not, however, enjoy the right to use any means they deem necessary to combat such threats, but must conduct themselves within the framework of international humanitarian and human rights law. Turkey has often failed in establishing that delicate balance between fighting a legitimate security threat and protecting individual rights, including the right to free expression as protected under Article 10 of the European Convention for the Protection of Human Rights.

Turkey's inability to balance the right of free expression with the exigencies of protecting territorial integrity has roots in the country's Ottoman past, when foreign powers—either directly or by supporting local minorities—whittled

---

[14]"Kendimi, devlete ve millete emanet ettim," *Hürriyet*, Istanbul (Internet Edition), December 12, 1997.

The Susurluk scandal, named after a town in western Turkey, involves the use by security forces of ultra nationalist gunmen to commit extrajudicial killings and other criminal acts. For more information, see section, "Violence Against Journalists."

[15]"Yargılanacaklar" ("They will be put on trial"), *Türkiye*, Istanbul, (Internet Edition), December 12, 1997. Mr. Bucak's exact words were, "Sonuna kadar devletçiyim."

[16]"Güvenli Tek Yer Vali Konutu" ("The only safe place is the governor's house"), *Radikal*, Istanbul, (Internet Edition), April 23, 1998. He and several other suspects were found guilty and sentenced to 5.5 years of imprisonment.

[17]Özbüdün, page 137.

away Ottoman lands. A 1997 indictment to close a pro-Kurdish party reflects this fear of dismemberment, which often views any reform or concession as the first step toward ruin:

> There is no doubt that there are different groups of people based on religion, race, language, and confession in many countries. Extending minority rights to all these groups could put the nation and national unity in danger. Demands for recognition of cultural identity based on affirming difference, have a tendency of separating from the whole over time. [18]

Even a recent Turkish parliamentary report on migration faced charges of "separatism" because it reportedly called for removing obstacles to private education, television, and radio broadcasts in Kurdish.[19]

---

[18]The indictment seeks to close the Democratic Mass Party (DKP). Ironically, the party's charter recognizes the territorial integrity of Turkey and pledges to uphold it. T.C. Cumhuriyet Başsavcılığı, *Iddianame*, (Republic of Turkey, Republic Head Prosecutors Office), Indictment SP.91 Hz.1997/138.

[19]"Göç raporu bölücülük suçlaması," ("Charges of Separatism against Migration Report"), *Milliyet* (Internet edition), January 26, 1998.

IV. INTERNATIONAL LEGAL OBLIGATIONS

Article 10 of the European Convention for the Protection of Human Rights

Turkey's primary legal obligation to protect freedom of expression is set out in the 1953 European Convention for the Protection of Fundamental Rights and Freedoms, which Turkey ratified in 1954 (Turkey is not a party to the International Covenant on Civil and Political Rights). In particular, Article 10 of the convention provides:

> 1. Everyone has the right to freedom of expression. This right shall include freedom to hold opinions and to receive and impart information and ideas without interference by public authority and regardless of frontiers. This Article shall not prevent States from requiring the licensing of broadcasting, television or cinema enterprises.

> 2. The exercise of these freedoms, since it carries with it duties and responsibilities, may be subject to such formalities, conditions, restrictions or penalties as are prescribed by law and are necessary in a democratic society, in the interests of national security, territorial integrity or public safety, for the prevention of disorder or crime, for the protection of health or morals, for the protection of the reputation or rights of others, for preventing the disclosure of information received in confidence, or for maintaining the authority and impartiality of the judiciary.

While protecting the right to freedom of expression, Article 10 allows tailored restrictions in the defense of, among other things, national security and territorial integrity. Any assessment of whether a given restriction violates Article 10 requires an evaluation of "whether a fair balance has been struck between the individual's fundamental right to freedom of expression and a democratic society's legitimate right to protect itself."[20] In addition, given the supreme importance placed on free expression, "the need for any restrictions must be established convincingly."[21] It is not enough for a government to show that the purpose of

---

[20]European Court of Human Rights, *Sunday Times* v. United Kingdom, Judgement of 26 April 1979, Series A, No. 30, Para. 59.

[21]Ibid.

limitations imposed was "useful," "reasonable," or "desirable;" instead, it must show that the measures met a "pressing social need."

In three recent cases, the European Court of Human Rights has issued judgments relating to free expression in Turkey. As stated above, the court was guided by the principle that a state may only restrict free expression under Article 10(2) where it can demonstrate a "pressing social need which would justify the finding that the interference complained of was 'proportionate to the legitimate aim pursued.'"[22] Applying these standards, the court ruled in two of the cases that Turkey had violated Article 10; in the third case, it found the restriction at issue to be permissible under Article 10(2).

In *Incal v. Turkey*, the court ruled that Turkey had violated Article 10 when it prosecuted members of the Izmir branch of a pro-Kurdish party in a national security court on terror charges for a leaflet it had prepared and submitted to authorities for approval to distribute.[23] The court stated,

> Subject to paragraph 2, it [Article 10] is applicable not only to "information" or "ideas" that are favourably received or regarded as inoffensive or as a matter of indifference, but also to those that offend, shock or disturb.... In order to demonstrate the existence of a "pressing social need" which would justify the finding that the interference complained of was "proportionate to the legitimate aim pursued," the representative of the Government asserted...that "it was apparent from the wording of the leaflet... that they were intended to foment an insurrection by one ethnic group against the State authorities." The court is prepared to take into account the background of the case submitted to it, particularly problems linked to the prevention of terrorism... . Here the court does not discern anything which would warrant the conclusion that Mr. Incal was in any way responsible for the problems of terrorism in Turkey, and more specifically Izmir.... In conclusion, Mr. Incal's conviction was disproportionate to the aim pursued, and therefore unnecessary

---

[22]European Court of Human Rights, Case of Incal v. Turkey, (41/1997/825/1031), Judgement, Strasbourg, 9 June 1998, paragraph 57.

[23]The leaflet was never distributed.

in a democratic society. There according has been a breach of Article 10 of the Convention.[24]

In *The Socialist Party and Others v. Turkey*, the court ruled that Turkey had violated Article 11, which protects freedom of association, when the Constitutional Court of Turkey ordered the closure of the Socialist Party (SP) in 1992.[25] The court closely linked Article 10's protection of free expression to the rights guaranteed in Article 11.[26] It explained:

> The Constitutional Court [of Turkey] noted that... Mr. Perinçek [the former head of the SP] had advocated the creation of minorities within Turkey and, ultimately, the establishment of a Kurdish-Turkish federation, to the detriment of the unity of the Turkish nation and the territorial integrity of the State.

> ...[T]he court has previously held that one of the principal characteristics of democracy is the possibility it offers of resolving a country's problems through dialogue, without recourse to violence.... Democracy thrives on freedom of expression.... Having analyzed Mr. Perinçek's statements, the court finds nothing in them that can be considered a call for the use of violence, an uprising or any other form of rejection of democratic principles.... Mr. Perinçek's statements, though critical and full of demands, did not appear to call into question the need for compliance with democratic principles and rules....In conclusion, the dissolution of the SP was disproportionate to the aim pursued and consequently unnecessary in a democratic society.[27]

---

[24]Incal v. Turkey, paragraphs 46, 57-59.

[25]European Court of Human Rights, The Case of the Socialist Party and Others v. Turkey, (20/1997/804/1007), Judgement, Strasbourg, 25 May 1998.

[26]In the case, the court ruled that, "notwithstanding its autonomous role and particular sphere of application, Article 11 must also be considered in light of Article 10. The protection of opinions and freedom to express them is one of the objectives of the freedom of assembly and association as enshrined in Article 11...." See Case of the Socialist Party and Others v. Turkey, paragraph 41.

[27]The Case of the Socialist Party and Others v. Turkey, paragraphs 43, 45, 46, 52, 54.

In *Zana v. Turkey*, however, the court ruled that Turkey had not violated the rights under Article 10 of Mr. Mehdi Zana, a leading Kurdish political figure and the former mayor of Diyarbakır, the largest city in southeastern Turkey, when it convicted him under terror charges in a state security court for making the statement, "I support the PKK national liberation movement; on the other hand, I am not in favor of massacres. Anyone can make mistakes, and the PKK killed women and children by mistake."[28]

The court noted that it was necessary to take into account the context in which the statement was made, explaining:

> The statement cannot, however, be looked at in isolation. It had a special significance in the circumstances of the case, as the applicant must have realized. As the court noted earlier... the interview coincided with murderous attacks carried out by the PKK on civilians in south-east Turkey, where there was extreme tension at the material time. In those circumstances the support given to the PKK—described as a "national liberation movement"—by the former mayor of Diyarbakır, the most important city in south-east Turkey, in an interview published in a major national daily newspaper, had to be regarded as likely to exacerbate an already explosive situation in the region. The court accordingly considers that the penalty imposed on the applicant could reasonably be regarded as answering a "pressing social need" and that the reasons adduced by the national authorities are "relevant and sufficient.... There consequently has been no breach of Article 10.[29]

Domestic Law

A host of laws that punish free expression exist in Turkey. Many are so loosely worded or broadly applied that they violate the principle, as defined by the European Court of Human Rights and outlined in the previous section, that

---

[28]European Court of Human Rights, Case of Zana v.Turkey, (69/1996/688/880), Judgement, Strasbourg, 25 November 1997, paragraph 12. The statement appeared in an interview published in the August 30, 1987, edition of *Cumhuriyet*, then a leading national daily published in Istanbul.

The court did rule, however, that Turkey had violated Mr. Zana's rights under Article 6, a fair trial.

[29]The Case of Zana v. Turkey.

restrictions of free expression under Article 10.2 must strike "a fair balance...between the individual's fundamental right to freedom of expression and a democratic society's legitimate right to protect itself" as well as meet a "pressing social need."

The 1982 constitution grants the right of free expression while at the same time qualifying the exercise of that right to an absurd degree. Its preamble states, for example,

> No protection shall be given to thoughts or opinions that run counter to Turkish national interests, the fundamental principle of the existence of the indivisibility of the Turkish state and territory, the historical and moral values of Turkishness, or the nationalism, principles, reforms, and modernism of Atatürk, and that as required by the principle of secularism there shall be absolutely no interference of sacred religious feeling in the affairs of state and politics.

Articles 26, 27, and 28 of the constitution, which grant, respectively, freedom of expression, science and art, and the press, contain more paragraphs limiting these rights than granting them.[30]

Some of the laws most frequently used to limit free expression include Articles 155, 158, 159, and 312 of the Penal Code, Article 8 of the 1991 Anti-Terror Law, and Law No. 5816, the "Law concerning crimes committed against Atatürk."

Article 159 of the Turkish Penal Code, one of the most widely employed laws, grants a "moral personality" (*manevî şahsiyeti*) both to corporate bodies, such as the judiciary and parliament, and to abstract concepts like "Turkishness." Article 159 warns that,

> Those who publicly insult or ridicule Turkishness, the Republic, the moral personality of Parliament, the Government, State Ministers, the military or security forces of the state, or the moral personality of the Judiciary will be punished with a penalty of no less than one year and no more than six years of maximum security imprisonment....[31]

---

[30]See Appendix, "Excerpts from Relevant Laws and Decrees."

[31]*Türk Ceza Kanunu* (Turkish Penal Code). This article was last amended in 1961.

In an official commentary on the law, a High Appeals Court (*Yargıtay*) judge argues that,

> The goal of this article [159] is to protect constitutional bodies (the Parliament, the lower house, the senate), the government, the ministers, public moral personalities (Turkishness, the Judiciary, the state military, security...forces....) from *all types of attack*; securing respect, together with the state's existence, honor, and identity for the state's highest bodies and the state's basic moral personalities is directly relevant and important. ....Therefore, the crimes listed in Article 159 carry a special importance and uniqueness among the crimes committed against state forces.[32]

Other penal code articles restricting free expression that purport to protect state bodies and their moral personalities include Article 155, "alienating people from military service," and Article 158, "insulting the president."[33]

---

[32]Italics added. Dr. Abdullah Pulat Gözübüyük, Yargıtay 8. Ceza Dairesi Başkanı, *Türk Ceza Kanunu Açılaması (An Explanation of the Turkish Penal Code)*, (Ankara: Kazancı Yayınevi, 1974), p. 620. Dr. Gözübüyük served as the head of the Eighth Criminal Office of the High Court of Appeals.

[33]Article 155 states that,

> Those who, except in circumstances indicated in the aforementioned articles, publish articles inciting people to break the law or harm the security of the country, or make publications or suggestions that make people unwilling to serve in the military or make speeches to that end in public meetings or gathering places, shall be imprisoned from between two months to two years and be punished with a heavy fine of between twenty-five and 200 lira.

Article 158 states that,

> Whoever insults the President of the Republic face-to-face or through cursing shall face a heavy penalty of not more than three years.... Even if the name of the President of the Republic is not directly mentioned, allusion and hint shall be considered as an attack made directly against the President if there is presumptive evidence beyond a reasonable doubt that the attack was made against the President of Turkey. If the crime is committed in any published form, the punishment will increase from one third to one half.

Another frequently used penal code article is 312.2, which prohibits "incit[ing] people to enmity and hatred by pointing to class, racial, religious, confessional, or regional differences."[34] Article 312.2 has largely been used against those writing about and debating the Kurdish question. In the absence of specific legislation prohibiting "Islamist propaganda," however, it has recently begun to be used against Islamists.[35]

Article 8 of the 1991 Anti-Terror Law outlaws "propaganda against the state's indivisibility."[36] Its scope was initially so wide—it took no account of intent or method—that even Turkey's greatest living writer, Yaşar Kemal, was prosecuted under it.[37] Article 8 of the Anti-Terror Law, before it was amended in 1995, stated that,

> *Regardless of method or intent,* written or oral propaganda along with meetings, demonstrations, and marches that have the goal of destroying the indivisible unity of the state with its territory and nation of the Republic of Turkey cannot be conducted.[38]

Article 15 of the State Civil Service Law, which prevents civil servants from speaking to the press, also aims to protect the state from outside scrutiny.

[34]Article 312 was amended by Law No. 2370 in October 1981, after the military coup of September 1980, to add paragraph two quoted above. Before the amendment, Article 312 made no mention of "racial, religious, confessional, or regional differences." The Article was clearly amended in reaction to the ethnic reawakening among many Kurds that came to the fore in the 1970s. In addition, Article 312.2 carried a heavier penalty, one to three years of imprisonment, than did Article 312.1, "praising a crime," which hitherto had mandated imprisonment of three months to one year. Imprisonment under Article 312.1 was also raised under Law No. 2370, to between six months and two years. See Gözübüyük, pp. 516-7, for the unamended version of Article 312.

[35]Until its was abolished by the Anti-Terror Law in 1991, Article 163.5 prohibited conducting propaganda using religion or religious symbols.

[36]The Anti-Terror Law was passed in April 1991, in part to replace Articles 141, 142, and 163 of the Penal Code. They, respectively, were used to prohibit Communist, Kurdish nationalist, and Islamist activities.

[37]Mr. Kemal was prosecuted for an article titled "Journey of Lies" (*Yalanlar Seferi*) that appeared in translation in the German news weekly *Der Spiegel*; eventually he was acquitted of this charge.

[38]Italics added. Unofficial translation. İsmail Malkoç and Mahmut Güler, *Ceza ve Yargılamada Temel Yasalar (Fundamental Laws in the Judiciary and Penal Code)*, (Ankara: Adil Yayınevi, 1994), p. 498. In such laws one encounters the same set phrase: "the indivisible unity of the state with its territory and nation" (*Devletin ülkesi ve milleti ile bölünmez bütünlüğü*).

Eager to win approval of a Customs Union deal with the European Union and embarrassed by the attention paid to cases like Mr. Kemal's, in October 1995 the government of then Prime Minister Tansu Çiller (DYP) pushed a bill through parliament amending Article 8 of the Anti-Terror Law. That amendment removed the phrase "regardless of method or intent." Consequently, eighty-two individuals charged under Article 8 were released.[39] Prosecutors, however, continued to open cases under the amended Article 8. The Yılmaz government presented a bill to parliament in the spring of 1998 that would liberalize Article 8.[40] It is currently pending.

Article 1.1 of Law No. 5816 penalizes, "anyone who publicly insults or curses the memory [of Atatürk]...with a sentence of between one and three years." [41] Law No. 5816 has primarily been used against Islamists, though mainstream intellectuals have also been sentenced under it.

---

[39]The amended Article 8, which still stands, states that,

Written or oral propaganda, along with meetings, demonstrations, and marches, that have the goal of destroying the indivisible unity of the state with its territory and nation of the Republic of Turkey cannot be conducted.

The amendment to Article 8 also reduced sentences from between two to five years to one to three years.

[40]Discussion with Dr. Hikmet Sami Türk, State Minister for Human Rights, Turkish Embassy, Washington, D.C., June 16, 1998. The draft law amending Article 8 apparently narrows the definition of the crime. Penal code Articles 7, 17, 159, and 312 are also included in the bill, which is presently on the agenda of the parliament's general assembly.

[41]The period of imprisonment is increased by one half if the act is carried out in the press.

V. FREEDOM OF EXPRESSION IN TURKEY TODAY

The Role of the Print Media

The media in Turkey today is caught between two contradictory roles. On the one hand, it tries, not without some success, to report news objectively and serve as a forum for public debate. Thanks to the hard work and dedication of a relatively small group of journalists, columnists, and editors, critical columns appear and unpleasant facts are reported under the arbitrary eye of state prosecutors. What is written in newspapers—despite their low daily circulation of only around three million—still counts. Şahin Alpay, a columnist for the daily *Milliyet*, commented that,

> Despite all the setbacks, if it weren't for the press, you couldn't talk about democracy or about pushing a liberalizing agenda. In the 1960s and 1970s, universities were the principal spokesmen for civil society, but they were put back in their place after the coups of 1971 and 1981. After 1980, it became the press that served as the voice for civil society.[42]

Another journalist acknowledged that the press, when it wishes, can make a difference.

> If the press wants to do something, it can. It does have some power. For the first three days after Metin Göktepe was murdered the papers wrote that he was killed under suspicious circumstances. But then most journalists, especially young ones, realized that the same could happen to them and started to pressure the higher ups to really investigate. It was completely through these efforts that the newspaper editors had to change their approach. At *Yeni Yüzyıl* fifteen of us told the directors that if the approach wasn't changed we would all resign.... If all events were followed like Göktepe, today things would be better.[43]

---

[42]Interview, Princeton, New Jersey, June 1998.

[43]Interview, Istanbul, September 1997. A photojournalist for the now defunct left-wing daily *Evrensel*, Metin Göktepe was beaten to death in police detention in January 1996. After much public outrage and dogged media coverage, five policemen charged in the case were convicted in March 1998 and sentenced to five years. Four others were acquitted.

A daily reading of the Turkish press bears out these observation, revealing an often lively and critical debate on any number of issues. Even commentary on the Kurdish conflict, a highly-charged and sensitive topic, is often critical and open. One study of the conflict noted that,

> All is not in solid conformity, however, even in the mainstream press. An important distinction has to be made between the reporting end of the news and columnists. Nearly every day in one paper or another—most often in the more liberal or intellectual papers, or even in the Islamist press—there are analyses or pieces by columnists who take a more critical and thoughtful approach to the Kurdish problem....[44]

On the other hand, the media often views itself as an advocate of state interests in general and a friend or a foe of a particular government. Economic dependence, many believe, lies at the root of this stance.[45] According to many journalists Human Rights Watch interviewed, more and more newspaper owners

---

The convictions, however, were overturned on appeal in July 1998. Another court ordered their retrial, and the men are presently on trial in Afyon in western Turkey.

[44]Henri J. Barkey and Graham E. Fuller, *Turkey's Kurdish Question* (Oxford, England: Rowman and Littlefield Publishers), 1998, p. 122.

[45]According to many interviewed for this report, media holding groups have increasingly moved away from the news as their main source of activity and income to other, more lucrative fields. They want a free hand to run their businesses as they see fit and in return offer, through favorable coverage, legitimization of the government and state.

Some pointed toward the recent unsuccessful attempt to amend the Radio and Television Broadcasting Law (RTÜK) as nothing more than an effort to legalize the recent purchase by media holding groups of state-owned electricity distribution networks. Under the present version of the RTÜK Law, individuals who own more than 10 percent of the shares in a media company are forbidden from taking part in public tenders, such as the privatization of the electricity distribution networks.

For a critical interpretation of the amendment to the RTÜK Law, see İlnur Çevik, "Why all the obstinacy to please media bosses," *Turkish Daily News*, Ankara, Internet Edition, May 8, 1998; İlnur Çevik, "Will the Parliament start working at last," *Turkish Daily News,* Internet Edition, May 18, 1998; Kemal Balcı, "Media barons block Parliament," *Turkish Daily News*, Internet Edition, May 26, 1998.

Those who defended the bill argued that it would introduce transparency and greater financial oversight. See Derya Sazak, "Şefaflık Korkusu" ("The Fear of Transparency"), *Milliyet*, Internet Edition, May 26, 1998.

have begun to play an unhealthy role in setting editorial policy. They are all too eager to fall into line to support official state policy, even at the cost of sacrificing journalistic ethics and standards. Mr. Alpay noted that,

> My experience in working in the Turkish press is that if a sensitive issue comes up, editors would say, "How would the authorities take this, how is this coordinated with Turkish national interests."[46]

One columnist at a mainstream Istanbul daily echoed these sentiments:

> Mainstream papers often see themselves as spokesmen for the state. They often use the first-person plural "We" voice. Many of our reporters, for example, talk to officials in a deferential way. They start a question by saying, "My General" or "My Minister", rather than "Mr. Minister" or "General." Once you establish that link, it is difficult to ask tough questions." Look at the emblems on, for example, *Sabah* or *Hürriyet*. When I was an editor at *Hürriyet* the reporter from Germany suggested that we remove the slogan on the front page "Turkey for Turks." For example, during the flag incident at the HADEP congress, the mainstream papers wrote headlines like, "If the state doesn't punish them, we will punish them."[47]

This tendency has only been exacerbated by increasing monopolization of the media. At present, two main holdings, the Doğan and Sabah groups, control between 65 and 70 percent of daily newspaper sales, depending upon circulation.[48]

---

[46]Interview, Princeton, New Jersey, June 1998.

[47]Interview, Istanbul, September 1997. About one-half of the estimated two million Turkish citizens who live in Germany are believed to be ethnic Kurds. In 1996, provocateurs ripped down the Turkish flag at the party congress of HADEP, a Kurdish nationalist party. In its place, they hung a PKK flag and a portrait of its leader, Mr. Abdullah Öcalan.

[48]Aydın Doğan, who heads a company bearing his name, owns three of Turkey's leading dailies that control about thirty-five percent of daily circulation: *Milliyet, Hürriyet, Radikal.* Dinç Bilgin of the *Sabah* group controls another 35 percent of newspaper circulation along with two mass-circulation dailies: *Sabah* and *Yeni Yüzyıl.* Each man also owns a television station.

Nazmi Bilgin, the head of the Ankara Journalists Association (*Ankara Gazeteciler Cemiyeti*) added that,

> There is a certain kind of censorship connected with monopolization. Two groups control 75 percent of readership. Monopolization is the twin sister of censorship....There is a certain level of self-censorship because of the relationship of owners and the state. I want anti-trust laws in Turkey to be passed.[49]

Deunionization has accompanied monopolization. Except for *Cumhuriyet*, the semi-official Anatolian News Agency, and two smaller press agencies, ANKA and ULUSAL, journalists and other press workers do not enjoy union representation. One journalist noted that,

> The Journalist Union still exists, but deunionization started in 1990 and 1991. People were pushed to resign from the union. It started at *Milliyet*. The newspapers simply do not want to have to conduct collective bargaining with their employees. Earlier all the papers had union representation.[50]

The Role of Private Television
Television was introduced in Turkey in 1963 with the establishment of the state-run Turkish Radio and Television (TRT).[51] In 1980, a second state-run channel was added, TRT-2. It broadcast in the periods when TRT was off the air.[52] In 1990, while on a visit to the United States, then President and former Prime Minister Turgut Özal announced that private foreign broadcasters could send

---

The rest of the market is divided among a number of national dailies of various ideological and editorial points of view. They include the following: *Cumhuriyet*, Kemalist intellectual; *Türkiye*, nationalist-conservative; *Akşam*, conservative; *Milli Gazete*, editorial support for Islamist Fazilet Party; *Akit*, radical Islamist; *Yeni Şafak*, Islamist intellectual; *Zaman*, mainstream Islamist. The local press in Turkey is generally weak or non-existent.

[49]Interview, Ankara, September 1997.

[50]Interview, Istanbul, September 1997. The individual asked that he remain anonymous.

[51]"An 'Idiot Box' or Instrument for Indoctrination," *Turkish Probe* (Ankara), April 12, 1996, p. 16.

[52]Ibid.

programs to Turkey via satellite despite a constitutional ban on private broadcasting.[53] At the time, Article 133 of the constitution gave the state-owned TRT a complete monopoly on radio and television broadcasting. Mr. Özal's son, Ahmet, quickly founded Turkey's first private television station, Magic Box, which began broadcasting from Germany. Soon a myriad of stations followed, preparing stories in Turkey but broadcasting them via satellite from abroad. By 1993 there were close to 700 private radio and television stations in Turkey despite their precarious legal status.[54] Finally, on July 8, 1993, parliament amended Article 133 of the constitution to permit private broadcasting in Turkey.[55]

The introduction of private television has undoubtedly increased the overall level of free expression—as well as the number of game shows, glitzy pop videos, and sensationalist reporting. Today the majority of Turks, like people all over the world, get their news from television. At present, there are sixteen national television stations—only four of which are state-owned—and another 360 local stations.[56] Dr. Haluk Şahin, a professor of communications and news coordinator of Kanal-D, a private television station, stated that,

> With the private channels, a lot changed. Old taboos were broken. Programing was shown that dealt with Islam, the Kurdish question, homosexuality, adultery. TV found that there was an audience. Free and more aggressive reporting was allowed. Anything went from early 1991 to mid-1994. There were no rules.[57]

Political talk shows lasting hours-on-end provided an unregulated forum to discuss Turkey's most pressing problems, whether Kurds or political Islam. One commentator noted that, "The past year [1994] has brought a revolution. In a country where the very word Kurd was taboo until a few years ago, millions tuned

---

[53]Ibid, p. 18.

[54]Ruhican Tul, "Radio Stations Hit the Ceiling," Turkish Probe, April 13, 1993, p. 19.

[55]The amended Article 133 states that: "Within a framework of conditions regulated by law, founding and running radio and television stations is free."

[56]"Promotion and Protection of the Right to Freedom of Opinion and Expression," report of the special rapporteur, Mr. Abid Hussain, submitted pursuant to the Commission on Human Rights Resolution 1996/53, United Nations, E/CN.4/1997/31. There are also 1,500 local radio stations.

[57]Interview, Istanbul, August 1997.

in two weeks ago to a no-holds-barred debate about the Kurdish question between top Turkish officials, Kurdish nationalists, and ordinary people that lasted nine hours until seven o'clock in the morning."[58]

Regulation, however, soon caught up with the free-wheeling private television senders in the form of the Radio and Television Law of April 13, 1994 (*RTÜK*).[59] Article 4 of the law mandates broadly-worded broadcasting principles and dictates sweeping restrictions. It states, among other things, that broadcasts cannot contradict, "the national and spiritual values of society" and "the general morality, civil peace, and structure of the Turkish family."[60] The law also prohibits

---

[58]Hugh Pope, "Broadcast Revolution in the Air for Turks," *The Independent*, London, January 14, 1995.

[59] The full name of the law is, "The Law Concerning the Founding and Broadcasts of Television and Radio/ Radyo ve Televizyonları n Kuruluş ve Yayınları Hakkında Kanun" (No. 3984). The law was published in the *Official Gazette* on April 20, 1994.

[60]Article 4 states that, "Radio and Television broadcasts are to be carried out in the understanding of public service according to the principles below:

Broadcasts cannot be contradictory to the following:

a) The existence and independence of the Turkish Republic, the indivisible unity of the state with its territory and nation;
b) The national and spiritual values of society....
d) The general morality, civil peace, and structure of the Turkish family....
g) The principle of not allowing broadcasts that create feelings of hatred in the community by encouraging violence and ethnic separatism;

Must be conducted in accordance with:

h) The general goals and basic principles of Turkish national education and the development of national culture;
I) Fairness and objectivity in broadcasting and the fundamental principle of respect for the law....
l) Presenting news in a speedy and correct way;
m) The principle that broadcasts will not be made that have a negative effect on the physical, intellectual, mental, and moral development of children and youth....
t) Radio and television broadcasts will be made in Turkish; however, for the purpose of teaching or of imparting news those foreign languages that have made a contribution to the development of universal cultural and scientific works can be used."

broadcasting in Kurdish.[61] A nine-member board, with five seats appointed by the government and four named by the opposition parties, implement the *RTÜK* law.

Radio and television stations face two penalties under the law: a warning and temporary closure. Article 33 allows the board to warn stations that violate provisions of Article 4; should the station violate a provision again, it can be closed temporarily for up to one year. Usually, the penalty consists of a one-day broadcast stop, which the station has a right to appeal in an administrative court. A bill amending the *RTÜK* law was recently presented by the Yılmaz government to the Turkish parliament. It appeared, however, to be targeted more at increasing the sphere of economic activity for owners of television stations than at increasing free expression. The bill was defeated.[62]

Almost all the national television stations—as well many of Turkey's 1,500 radio stations—have been closed down for various periods, causing revenue loss and reduction in market share. On any given day, it is not uncommon to see a black screen on television with the words, "Closed by order of *RTÜK*." On June 20, 1997, the daily *Milliyet* reported that eight television stations and two radio stations have been given closure penalties.[63] A major broadcaster, Kanal D, had the following record of warnings and closures: 1994, five warnings; 1995, two closures and five warnings; 1996, ten closures and five warnings; 1997, six closures; 1998, thirteen closures.[64] Many of these penalties were handed down for violating either Article 4d of the law, which states that broadcasts must be made in context of "the general morality, civil peace, and structure of the Turkish family," or Article 4m, which prohibits broadcasts that a "negatively affect the physical, mental, psychological, or moral development of children and youth." Sometimes closure is the result of a politically-charged broadcast. A local television station in

---

[61]For more on this see, "Restrictions on the Use of the Kurdish Language."

[62]See section, "The Role of Print Media" for a greater discussion of this draft law. In September 1997, the Press Council of Turkey gave the Justice Ministry a draft bill amending the RTÜK Law. There was also talk of changing the law to substitute fines for the closing of stations. See "TV, Radio Broadcasting Principles Revised," *Turkish Daily News*, Ankara, September 20, 1997; Sungurlu Receives Press Council's Draft New RTUK Law," *Turkish Daily News*, September 11, 1997.

[63]"TV'lere ceza yağdı" ("Penalties Rain Down on Television Stations"), *Milliyet* (Internet version), June 20, 1997. ATV, Cine-5, Show-TV, Kanal E, HBB, Kanal 7, and Kanal 6, all television stations, were all closed for a day; Interstar TV was closed for two days. Şok Radio was closed for a day, while Radio Hedef was closed for four days.

[64]Interview with Şenol Caner, Legal Adviser, Kanal D, Istanbul, August 1997. Records from Kanal D's Legal Office, January 1999.

Diyarbakır, Metro TV, was closed for one month in January 1998 after broadcasting a program featuring interviews with relatives of PKK security detainees who had taken part in a hunger strike.[65] Metro TV was closed for violating Article 4g, "the principle of not allowing broadcasts that create feelings of hatred in the community by encouraging violence and ethnic separatism."

All journalists whom Human Rights Watch interviewed criticized the *RTÜK* Law and its effect on broadcasting. Oktay Ekşi, editor-in-chief of *Hürriyet* and the director of the Press Council, stated that," You must have legislation to change RTÜK. At present, political will shapes it. Its board consists of nine members: five from the government parties and four from the opposition. It must be completely independent."[66] Şenol Caner, legal council for Kanal D, complained about the imprecise wording of the law: "We are always walking on thin ice because many of these prohibitions are so vaguely worded."[67]

At present, private television still provides an important forum for debate, along with the usual soft news programing and fluff found on commercial television stations around the globe. Thanks to the RTÜK laws and other politically-inspired restrictions, however, private broadcasting has lost a large degree of its earlier luster and near absolute freedom. A producer for a popular news program summed up the present situation in the following way:

> The contribution of private TV. The fact that there are seven or eight or however many private television stations doesn't show that there is freedom of expression. It is appropriate to me. We have one of the best news programs in television. We try to do things in a Western way....We have a lot of information and we do respectable work...[But] sometimes we have to say things indirectly. The bosses of the program have to make a decision. Do we show everything or do we pull back. Two out of three programs will send people's eyes out of their heads; one we pull back on.[68]

---

[65]"Turkey Closes TV station for Kurd Rebel Programme," Reuters, January 19, 1998.

[66]Interview, Istanbul, August 1997.

[67]Interview, Istanbul, August 1997.

[68]Interview, Turkey, November 1997. The individual requested anonymity because he is not the executive producer for the program and did not have permission to speak ex officio for the show.

Fehmi Koru, the chief columnist at the daily *Zaman*, believed the influence of private television had largely been positive until early 1997, when the military began to play a more open role in politics. According to him,

> If you asked me three to four months ago about private television, I would have said yes. All gave credence to new ideas and new thoughts. People learned things on the news programs. But in the past four to five months, all stay more or less in line with the official line.[69]

The Role of the Military

The military today sees itself as the defender of the Kemalist republic and all it stands for. Supported by trade unions, the press, and big business, the military ousted the Islamist-led government of Prime Minister Necmettin Erbakan in June 1997. Since that time, the military has not left the political scene. In its fight against "fundamentalism," the military today plays a greater role in day-to-day politics than at any time since the restoration of civilian rule on December 24, 1983.

The army wields its influence mainly through the National Security Council (*Milli Güvenlik Kurulu-MGK*), a half-civilian/half-military organ chaired by the president and provided for under Article 118 of the constitution.[70] The MGK gives the military a voice on matters "with regard to the formulation, establishment, and implementation of the national security policy of the state."[71] "National securit·' policy" is understood to include almost all issues, both foreign and domestic.

---

[69]Interview, Ankara, September 1997. In early 1997, the General Staff of the Turkish military began to pressure the then Islamist-led government of Prime Minister Necmettin Erbakan over what it deemed the government's Islamic policies. On June 18, 1997, Prime Minister Erbakan resigned under intense military pressure. See following section, "The Role of the Military."

[70] In addition to the president, the MGK includes the prime minister, the ministers of defense, foreign affairs, and the interior, as well as the chief of the General Staff and all major military commanders, including the commander of the gendarmerie. The body meets monthly.

To track Islamists, the military has also created purely military bodies, such as the "Western Working Group" (*Batı Çalışma Grubu*). Former Prime Minister Yılmaz unsuccessfully tried to force the military to disband the organization.

[71]Article 118.3

Not surprisingly, the high-profile role of the military has had a negative effect on the freedom of the press and the media. Pressure can come directly or indirectly. In November 1997, the National Security Council called on the Supreme Radio and Television Board (RTÜK) to crack down on the burgeoning number of private Islamist radio and television stations.[72] In March 1998, Yaşar Kaplan, a columnist for the radical, pro-Islamist daily *Akit,* was arrested and remanded into custody on charges that he violated Article 95.4-5 of the Military Penal Code prohibiting "press crimes aimed at poisoning hierarchial military relations."[73] That same month, the Office of the General Staff banned Mehmet Ali Birand, Yalçın Doğan, and Muharrem Sarıkaya from entering military bases or from speaking with members of the military, reportedly because of their reporting.[74] In April, alleged testimony from a captured PKK field commander, Şemdin Sakık, fingered Birand and another columnist, Cengiz Çandar, as "PKK stooges." The unsubstantiated and highly improbable charges would most likely not have been leaked without the permission of the army, which captured Sakık and took part in his interrogation. The daily *Sabah,* for which both men worked, suspended Mr. Çandar temporarily and forced out Mr. Birand.

Human Rights Watch has also heard first-hand reports from several mainstream, respected journalists concerning the military's heavy-handed pressure against those it perceives as troublesome or as not fully supporting the drive against "fundamentalism." Some have even asserted that the Office of the General Staff has begun to keep files on journalists, noting the tone and content of their reporting and columns. One reporter stated that,

---

[72]*Hürriyet*, November 24, 1997; "Council Asks Turk Government to Hit Islamic Media," Reuters, November 26, 1997. The National Security Council charged that these stations were airing broadcasts that, "conflict with the constitutionally inviolable principles of the state."

[73]*TİHV: Türkiye'de Basın Özgürlüğü (Human Rights Foundation of Turkey: Press Freedom in Turkey),* March 1998, pp. 5-8, p. 11; "Turkish Islamist Reporters Face Eight Years in Jail," Reuters, May 21, 1998. In Turkey, civilians can be tried in military courts if they violate provisions of the military penal code.

[74]All three are long-time, respected journalists. Mr. Birand has written widely on the military, including works on the institution *Shirts of Steel (Emret Komutanım)* and on the 1980 coup, *The Generals' Coup in Turkey (12 Eyül saat 04.00).* The order was lifted shortly after it was issued.

In late March or April General Çevik Bir, who was then Deputy Chief of Staff, went to Istanbul to the office of our publisher, Aydın Doğan, with a folder of articles that he did not like. He also had a number of names of journalists with whom he was displeased. After that my editor called me on the phone and said, "Be careful."[75]

Human Rights Watch is aware of at least one case in which a career journalist, Koray Düzgören, a former writer and editor of the "Forum" page of the daily *Radikal,*was fired after his editors received pressure from military authorities.[76] Mr. Düzgören apparently ran afoul of the military because of his critical writing on the Kurdish question and because of his assertions that the military—as well as the police—were implicated in the Susurluk scandal.[77] According to Mr. Düzgören,

> *Radikal* started to publish in October 1996. The paper glowed because of its earnest publishing about the gangs that were uncovered following the Susurluk incident. Circulation increased. But, later, when all the big media groups joined the campaign to force Refah out of power, *Radikal* was no exception....It turned out that writing and criticism distant to state discourse were not approved. The military was not to be criticized. This situation was openly communicated to the writers by the paper's administrators. It was stated that the military kept files for some journalists either at the National Security Council or the General Staff and gave grades on performance; we were told that, "In the past few days *Radikal*'s grades have been falling a lot...." On March 2, I was told the following by the General Director of the paper: "We know that you have been successful, and the affair doesn't stem from you. Your writing at this paper is not wanted by the military....The owner of the paper, Aydın Doğan, could not do anything about this demand.

---

[75]Interview, August 1998, by phone to Istanbul. Individual requested anonymity.

[76]Information for this section comes from phone interviews with Mr. Düzgören and from material Mr. Düzgören sent Human Rights Watch. Mr. Düzgören was also interviewed for this report in Istanbul in August and September 1997.

[77]In November 1997, Mr. Düzgören published a collection of his columns written at *Radikal* and at *Yeni Yüzyıl, Excuse us for the Gangs (Çeteden özür diliyoruz).*

Therefore you are not going to write anymore. We apologize for
this and for the unexpectedness of the situation."

After a thirty-year career as a journalist in the mainstream press, Mr. Düzgören is
unable to find work in his profession.

VI. VIOLENCE AGAINST JOURNALISTS

Political Killings

Between 1992-95, politically-motivated killings resulting from the Kurdish conflict engulfed Turkey. Journalists were not exempt from this violence. During this period, twenty-nine reporters were murdered in Turkey, the overwhelming majority in the southeast or for reasons connected with the conflict there.[78] Of the twenty-nine murdered journalists, one died under suspicious circumstances in police detention, one was shot by a police armored car at the time of unrest during the Nevroz festival in 1992, one was murdered for unknown reasons, five were believed killed by the PKK, two were murdered by the far-left armed group "Revolutionary Left" (Dev-Sol), one was murdered by the far-right armed group İBDA-C (Islamic Great Eastern Raiders-Front) in a bombing attack, and eighteen were the victims of "actor unknown murders" (*faili meçhul cinayetleri*). Many of these "actor unknown" murders are believed to be carried out by groups allegedly linked to security forces or acting with the connivance of the police.[79] The vast majority of those killed in "actor unknown murders" worked for Kurdish-nationalist papers such as *Özgür Gündem* and *Özgür Ülke*.

Murder of non-combatants became an art practiced by all, including by shadowy groups believed to be acting in concert with or with the connivance of security officials or by the PKK. The PKK committed politically-motivated murders to eliminate opposing political groups within the Kurdish community and to intimidate those who cooperated with the state, such as civil servants, teachers, or village guard members and their families. Between 1992 and 1995, the height of political violence, the PKK committed at least 768 politically-motivated

---

[78]Five died in Istanbul, and one each in Ankara, Bursa, Gebze, and Kırıkkale. The remaining twenty were killed in southeastern Turkey.

[79] Information on murdered journalists comes from the annual report or other reports of the Human Rights Foundation of Turkey (*Türkiye İnsan Hakları Vakfı-TİHV*). See *1992 Türkiye İnsan Hakları Raporu,* p. 82 and pp. 143-148; *1993 Türkiye İnsan Hakları Raporu,* pp. 230-236; *1994 Turkey Human Rights Report,* pp. 247-253; *1995 Turkey Human Rights Report,* pp. 320-1; *TİHV: Türkiye'de Basın Özgürlüğü (Human Rights Foundation of Turkey: Press Freedom in Turkey),* March 1998, pp. 5-8. Fourteen of the murders took place in 1992, eight in 1993, five in 1994, and one in 1995. Since 1996, one journalist was murdered: Metin Göktepe, reporter for the now closed *Evrensel,* was beaten to death in Istanbul in police detention in January 1996. İhsan Karakuş, the owner of *Silvan,* a local paper in the Silvan district of Diyarbakır, was murdered in March 1992 for unknown reasons. Mr. Karakuş had a reputation as a political neutral, and no group took responsibility for the murder.

37

murders.[80] In order to show its strength among the local population, the PKK usually took responsibility for these killings.

The "actor unknown murders" (*faili meçhul cinayetleri*) struck large numbers of individuals believed sympathetic to Kurdish-nationalist aspirations, whether those fighting for minority rights for Kurds or alleged PKK members and sympathizers. Politicians from the pro-Kurdish parties, intellectuals, lawyers who took PKK cases, doctors suspected of treating wounded PKK fighters, businessmen believed to be channeling funds to the PKK, and journalists at far-left or Kurdish-nationalist publications all fell victim, as did the urban and rural cadres of the PKK. Often the attacks took place in broad daylight, even in the center of provincial capitals. Victims were killed with a single shot to the head or after being kidnapped and tortured. Few individuals were ever brought to trial for these killings. Between 1992 and 1995, at least 1,288 individuals are believed to have been murdered in such attacks.[81]

While definitive guilt—in the absence of an investigation of each killing—cannot yet be assigned for the "actor unknown murders," evidence uncovered by—among others—two Turkish parliamentary commissions and a 1997 investigation by the prime minister's office points toward either direct or indirect state involvement in a number of incidents. Security forces are believed to have used captured PKK members who turned state's evidence—so-called confessors (*itirafçi*)— to commit these killings. In other cases, police are alleged to have simply turned a blind eye as enemies of the PKK, such as the radical Islamist *Hezbullah*, conducted attacks. Even when state authorities arrested those believed involved in such killings, such as the widescale round-up of *Hezbullah* members in 1995-1996, little was done to explore links to security forces.

In 1995, a special commission of the Turkish parliament issued a report on "actor unknown killings." The commission was formed in 1993, after the car bomb murder of the popular investigative journalist, Uğur Mumcu. While the commission did not directly charge that the state conducted a policy of assassination or was knowingly involved in such killings, the 328-page report

---

[80] 214 in 1992; 294 in 1993; 193 in 1994; 67 in 1995. The figure is based on information contained in the section, "Organization Executions" (*Örgüt Infazları*) of the Annual Reports of the Human Rights Foundation of Turkey for the period 1992-1995. The figure cited above does not include indiscriminate fire attacks by the PKK during military operations and the mass targeting of civilians during raids on villages.

[81] 267 in 1992; 429 in 1993; 423 in 1994; 169 in 1995. The figure is based on information contained in the section, Unknown Actor Murders (*Faili Meçhul Cinayetler*) of the Annual Reports of the Human Rights Foundation of Turkey for the period 1992-1995.

stated that security officials, village guards, and confessors acting "as individuals" had been involved in some of the "actor unknown killings" and gave concrete examples.[82] Certain parts of the report, however, seem to go farther by way of inference and raise serious questions that are left unanswered. According to the report:

> Actor unknown political murders are usually committed in the middle of the street, in the city's busiest places and in broad daylight. The fact is that the perpetration of murders committed in broad daylight in the city's busiest districts elicits fear and suspicion among the citizens. The fact that perpetrators of politically-motivated murders cannot be captured is perceived by the citizen as the state turning a blind eye to these murders in light of the fact that security forces capture or determine the perpetrators of murders carried out in criminal cases within a short period. Thus the organization [PKK] uses this very cleverly and conducts propaganda along these lines. If the state wants the trust of the citizens, at the desired moment it must be able to capture or determine the perpetrators of these crimes. If actor unknown murders are committed and their perpetrators cannot be found in a small district like Silopi or in the busiest streets of the districts like Silvan and Batman, the impression arises that these [actors] cannot be determined because the state does not want to. The citizens do not serve as witnesses because of the widespread propaganda conducted [by the PKK] alleging that the state committed the actor unknown political murders and because of the fact that in the beginning the fate of citizens who were witnesses...was also to become victims of actor unknown political murders... Despite the fact that there was a killing, a citizen's relatives and friends are afraid to serve as witnesses in killings committed in a coffee house in front of twenty or thirty

---

[82]See the committee's report, *T.B.M.M. Faili Meçhul Cinayetler Araştırma Komisyonu Raporu (Taslak)* (Report of the Turkish Parliament Actor Unknown Murder Investigation Commission (Draft). The report was later published unedited by a small left-wing party, the United Socialist Party (BSP), in July 1995. In June 1995, Human Rights Watch also interviewed the commission's chairman, M. Sadık Avundukluoğlu, True Path Party (DYP) deputy. He admitted that security officers and others were involved in the killings "as individuals."

people in murders committed in the busiest center of a town. The state remains under suspicion because individuals known as "Hezbullah" conduct an operation and then cannot be captured in a region where even the PKK organization which has created urban committees cannot carry out an operation in broad daylight in the town's busiest street.[83]

The so-called "Susurluk scandal" reignited the public debate concerning the state's role in "actor unknown killings" and its use of extrajudicial methods. On November 3, 1996, a car loaded with weapons, silencers, and passports issued in false names crashed head-on with a truck near the district town of Susurluk in western Turkey. Aside from its strange cargo, the vehicle transported an even stranger group of passengers: Hüseyin Kocadağ, the head of the Istanbul Police Academy; Abdullah Çatlı, an ultra-right wing (*ülkücü*) militant wanted by Interpol and indicted for seven politically-motivated killings committed in 1978; Gonca Us, allegedly Mr. Çatlı's girlfriend; and Sedat Bucak, an ethnic Kurdish parliamentarian and Kurdish tribal leader. Mr. Bucak's tribe supplies a large number of village guards in the state's fight against the PKK. All but Mr. Bucak were killed in the accident.[84] Shortly after the compromising incident, the parliament organized a commission to conduct an investigation. While the commission's report proved somewhat disappointing, some of the evidence given before it—which was later published as a two-volume book—did not.[85]

---

[83]Ibid, page 78-79. Even state officials were intimidated. The report relates an incident in which the security director of Batman province was apparently removed from his office after he reported to the commission allegations of interaction between Hezbullah and a military unit in the province. The report complains that after this incident other public officials were reticent in talking: "The end of the public official who made statements to our commission on several topics and who reported things sincerely (*samimi*) was to be removed from office." See pages 80-81.

[84]As this report was going to press, yet another Susurluk-like gang scandal rocked Turkey. After the August 1998 arrest in France of a wanted Turkish ultra nationalist gunman, Alaatin Çakıcı, it was discovered that Mr. Çakıcı had been in phone contact with a state minister, Mr. Eyüp Aşık of the ruling Motherland Party (ANAP). It was even alleged that Mr. Aşık had helped the right-winger escape capture. For his part, the ANAP minister denied wrongdoing.

[85]The Ankara-based English-language news and economics weekly *Briefing* complained that the report presented "crimes but no criminals." See "Susurluk Back on the Streets," *Briefing*, April 7, 1997.

Hanefi Avcı, who worked in the intelligence branch of the Diyarbakır Security Directorate from 1984 to 1992 and later served as the assistant director of the General Security Directorate Intelligence, testified that some in the security apparatus began to seek out "extrajudicial" methods of combating the PKK. According to him, the state faced a dilemma. Normal methods, i.e., arresting those believed to have committed offenses and putting them on trial, proved less than effective in fighting the PKK. Mr. Avcı testified that,

> Sir, my observations are like this: In the heads of some security officials there was [the belief] or some such feeling that the state could not sufficiently fight against the serious attacks of the PKK and against some PKK members and individuals who were giving large-scale support to the PKK using merely legal means. So you see, you have some people giving large-scale support to the PKK and they are captured. Sufficient evidence, however, cannot be brought against them and they are let go. Or, you have a few people who are giving quite a bit of intelligence to the PKK and because of that quite a few officials are being martyred. Again, however, you could not conduct a proper legal proceeding. At that time some state officials began to believe in the need to fight this with a different kind of struggle, in the necessity to do one's duty with a new kind of understanding, more accurately put, in the necessity to conduct one's duty acting outside the law and outside the legal system....[86]

The commission had no power to indict and dissolved itself in April 1998 after the report appeared.

In January 1998, an investigative committee under the prime minister issued its own Susurluk report. Then Prime Minister Mesut Yılmaz released the report, written by Kutlu Savaş, in a somewhat censored form.[87] While the report is

---

[86]Veli Özdemir, *İfade Tutanakları: Susurluk Belgeleri 1 (Testimony Minutes: The Susurluk Documents 1)*, (Istanbul:Scala Publishing, April 1997). The book is the verbatim testimony of individuals who testified before the Susurluk Commission of the Turkish Parliament. A second volume came out in October 1997.

[87]Twelve pages of the 120-page report were blacked out. The report was published as a free insert by the Istanbul daily *Radikal*. See, *Kutlu Savaş'ın hazırladığı Susurluk Raporu* (The Susurluk Report Prepared by Kutlu Savaş).

less than comprehensive, it admitted that security forces had teamed up with some organized crime figures and ultra-right wing nationalists to "eliminate" ethnic Kurdish businessmen, drug dealers, and others believed to be financing the PKK. The report alleges that, "The beginning of the Susurluk event could even perhaps be hidden in a sentence of then Prime Minister Tansu Çiller, who said 'We have in our hands a list of businessmen helping the PKK.' After that the executions started."[88] The report states that such operations also took the life of the ethnic Kurdish writer and journalist Musa Anter, murdered in 1992. The report admits, however, that "the decision to kill [Anter] was a mistake."[89] The report laconically admits that, "Other journalists were killed." Unfortunately, the section immediately after this sentence is censored.

Beatings and Other Violence

Beatings and other violence against journalists—especially when covering demonstrations or in southeastern Turkey—is largely a function of two factors: the poor training of police; and, more importantly, an increasing politicization of the security forces.

After the 1980 coup, an attempt was made to depoliticize the police force, which had splintered into rival right- and left-wing unions, *Pol-Bir and Pol-Der*.[90]

---

[88]*Susurluk Raporu*, p. 11.

[89]*Susurluk Raporu*, p. 61.

[90]In addition, before the coup, a network of unofficial links between police and ultra-right wing national groups, so-called "idealists" or "*ülkücü*' existed.

Ultra-nationalists, or *ülkücü*, are usually associated with the National Action Party (*Milli Hareket Partisi-MHP*), a right-wing, pan-Turkic, radical nationalist party that was represented in the Turkish Parliament until the December 1995 elections, when it received only 8 percent of the vote, failing to pass the 10 percent barrier necessary for parliamentary representation. Its leader is Alpaslan Türkeş, a retired army colonel who played a major role during Turkey's 1960 coup.

From 1975-1977, the predecessor to MHP, also headed by Türkeş, was a junior partner in Suleyman Demirel's coalition National Front government where he served as deputy prime minister. At the time there were numerous allegations that Türkeş placed his supporters in the security apparatus. The *Ülkücü Gençlik Derneği*, ÜGD, ["Idealist Youth Association"], which functioned as a youth branch for MHP, carried out some of the extremist right-wing terror of the 1970s. Feroz Ahmad, a noted scholar of this period, commented in his 1993 work *The Making of Modern Turkey*, that, "Meanwhile, the Grey Wolves [*ülkücü*], with Türkeş as deputy premier, also saw themselves as part of the state and operated with greater confidence in creating a climate of terror designed to intimidate their opponents." The *ülkücü* fought radical leftist groups who also used terror tactics in the

Unfortunately, while leftists were purged from police ranks, ultra-rightists remained. In addition, it appears that Islamists—especially graduates of İmam-Hatip religious high schools—were increasingly recruited into police ranks. [91]

Security forces—especially those involved in actions against the PKK or armed radical leftist groups—have seemingly cultivated a tight, if largely unofficial, relationship with ultra-nationalist right-wing groups, so-called "ülkücü," or "idealists."[92] In addition, many police sympathize with far-right nationalist or Islamist groups. Kemal, a former policeman who was expelled from the force for contact with an outlawed left-wing group, complained that,

> What they tell you at the police school and what you do on the job are two different things. At the school they taught us about human rights, but at demonstrations—I was a riot policeman for three years with the riot police ("Çevik Kuvvetleri")—they would tell us to beat the people if it was a leftist protest but to show restraint if they were rightists or Islamists. There were two standards: if you capture a religious person, one standard, but if you capture a leftist, you beat him. About eighty or ninety percent of the police in my unit were MHP or fundamentalist.[93]

---

political violence that plagued Turkey in the 1970s. Over 5,000 were killed in right/left terror in the years immediately preceding the September 12, 1980, military coup.

    After the 1980 coup, Türkeş was arrested and his party closed down. MHP was reestablished after a ban on pre-coup parties and politicians was lifted. The ülkücü groups are active today and often battle leftist or Kurdish groups, though at a much lower level than the fighting of the 1970s. Some prominent members of the ülkücü movement later entered mainstream politics in the 1980s and 1990s. Muhsin Yazıcıoğlu, chairman of the far-right "Great Unity Party" (Büyük Birlik Partisi), which has seven seats in parliament, was active in the ÜGD in the 1970s.

    [91]See a three-part series by Erbil Tüşalp on politicization in the police force that appeared in the daily Radikal from August 1-3, 1997.

    [92]The following three paragraphs are reprinted with minor edits from the March 1997 Human Rights Watch Report, "Turkey: Torture and Mistreatment in Pre-Trial Detention by the Anti-Terror Police."

    [93]Human Rights Watch/Helsinki interview, October 1995, pp. 30-31. See also "Kemal" in section, "Interview with Detainees," Human Rights Watch Report, "Turkey: Torture and Mistreatment in Pre-Trial Detention by the Anti-Terror Police," March 1997, p. 18.

Recep Ordulu, who served as the assistant security director in Istanbul before the 1980 coup, concurred with his opinion:

> A person falls to the ground, but they keep beating. The police have the authority to use force, but they shouldn't exceed this....Actions by certain groups are seen as guilty, while others are met with tolerance. You know the police have one attitude for those who protest outside the Israeli Embassy and another one for left-wing groups.[94]

In July 1996, the liberal Istanbul daily *Cumhuriyet* compared the police reaction to demonstrations by the leftist civil servant union *KESK*, which was met with night sticks and attacked, and one by the right-wing union *KAMU-SEN*, which received a friendly greeting from police.[95]

A 1995 report prepared by the center-left Republican People's Party (CHP), at the time the junior partner in the government of Prime Minister Tansu Çiller, criticized the increasing influence of extreme right-wing and fundamentalist groups among the security forces. Such groups are usually ideologically hostile to Kurdish and left-wing organizations, the groups police deal with most often in security cases. The report presented the following conclusions: of the seventy-seven provincial security directors, 48 percent were alleged to be either radical fundamentalists (*köktendinci*) or extreme nationalists (*ülkücü*); police academies and "special team" training centers only accept those with a "nationalist" reference because only "nationalists fight against terror;" only 18 percent of the provincial security directors could be considered "democrats;" the police had a mentality to consider all those not from their ranks as the enemy.[96] One scholar commented that, "Young right-wing hoodlums, who once carried out raids against "leftist" tea houses, now became policemen and schoolteachers or were recruited into the special forces fighting the Kurdish guerrillas."[97]

---

[94] Çizmeci, *Milliyet*, Istanbul, July 1995. See also Human Rights Watch Report, "Turkey: Torture and Mistreatment in Pre-Trial Detention by the Anti-Terror Police," March 1997, p. 31.

[95] "Kamu-Sen Eylemi: Sağ Sendikaya Polisten Hoşgörü," *Cumhuriyet*, Istanbul, July 5, 1996.

[96] "Müthiş Raporu", *Milliyet*, September 22, 1995, p.1-8.

[97] Martin Van Bruinessen, "Kurds, Turks and the Alevi Revival in Turkey," *MERIP*, Summer 1996, p. 8.

Other sources make the same charges. In August 1994, Şevket Kazan, the former justice minister from the Islamist Welfare (*Refah*) Party, charged that most members of the "special teams," noted for their abusive behavior in southeastern Turkey, were members of the far right Nationalist Action Party (*Milliyetçi Hareket Partisi-MHP*).[98] In the fall of 1996, the headquarters of the General Staff prepared a brochure for internal distribution to all security forces in the southeast titled, "Public Relations and Winning the People in Internal Security."[99] In a warning directed at "special team members," the brochure called on security force members not to wear or make symbols of a "definite political nature that incites the populace;" implied was the "grey wolf" and three crescent symbols associated with MHP and ülkücü groups.[100] During an investigation of the Sivas massacre of 1993, when fundamentalists burned down a hotel killing thirty-seven Alevi intellectuals, a Turkish parliamentary investigation committee discovered that Islamist bulletins faxed to local newspapers and believed to have provoked the public to violence were sent from the Sivas Security Directorate.[101]

Many journalists, in contrast, especially younger ones, tend to support left-wing or liberal political parties or beliefs. Research conducted by the Contemporary Journalists Association in 1994 indicated that most journalists in Turkey leaned to the left. In response to the question—"Which political inclination...are you closest to?"— journalists polled gave the following answers: 8 percent, conservative; 23 percent, liberal; 51 percent, social democratic; 14 percent, socialist; 1 percent, communist; two percent, other.[102]

Consequently, police often view reporters as ideological enemies who "meddle" in police affairs, especially those who work for leftist publications. The case of Metin Göktepe, who worked as a photojournalist for the now defunct left-wing daily *Evrensel*, represents an example of such an encounter.[103] He was beaten to death in police detention in January 1996, after having been detained while covering a funeral for far-left prisoners killed in a prison riot.

Mr. Göktepe was taken into custody along with two journalists from mainstream dailies, who were later released. Initially the prosecutor in the case

---

[98]"Özel Tim MHP militanı," *Cumhuriyet*, Istanbul, August 25, 1994.

[99]"Genelkurmay'dan özel time uyarı," *Milliyet,* Istanbul, September 25, 1996.

[100]Ibid.

[101]Jan Pacal, "Police File, 1," Turkish Daily News, Ankara, July 8, 1996.

[102]M. Kemal Öke, *Gazeteci: Türkiye'de Basın Çalışanları Üzerine Bir İnceleme (Journalist: A Study of those Working in the Press in Turkey)*, (Ankara: ÇGD Publishing, December 1994), p. 62. Out of 289 polled, 253 responded.

[103]*Evrensel* was known as a radical-left, though not extreme left, publication.

stated that Gőktepe had been released and died in a nearby park, while then Istanbul Security Director Orhan Taşanlar denied that the journalist had even been detained by police.[104] In fact, Gőktepe was detained at noon on January 8, 1996, in Istanbul while covering a funeral of prisoners reportedly beaten to death during prison unrest. Other reporters witnessed his detention and other detainees reported speaking to him. Police detained roughly 1,000 individuals and held them in a sport center turned into a temporary holding facility. Gőktepe's body was discovered roughly eight hours later at a snack bar near the sports facility. An autopsy indicated that Gőktepe died of internal bleeding to the brain and body due to blows.[105]

In April 1998, anti-terror police on trial for the death of a suspect in their custody attacked journalists, bystanders, and defense lawyers after they were found guilty.[106] When riot police stationed outside entered the court room, they too began to beat the journalists and lawyers.[107] Although the Ministry of the Interior conducted an investigation into the incident, its findings have not been made public. Both the police and the victims of the beatings filed appeals at the Council of State (Danistay). As of January 1999, the case was still pending.[108]

During demonstrations, especially by Islamists or right-wing groups, police often harass journalists. After a recent Islamist demonstration, one commentator noted that,

> ...Scenes of police savagely billy-clubbing young men or dragging females along the ground by the hair so familiar in leftist demonstrations were absent last Tuesday....police showed the utmost restraint to these demonstrators, and received their reward with chants of appreciation and solidarity from the

---

[104]Hűlya Topcu, "Katiler hâlâ aramızda," *Cumhuriyet Hafta*, January 10, 1997. Unless otherwise cited, background information concerning the Gőktepe case comes from this article.

[105]After more than two years and as a result of a massive public outcry, five police officers were convicted of "manslaughter" in the case and each given 7.5 years of imprisonment; six others were acquitted. In July 1998, however, an appeals court overturned the convictions, and the men are presently being retried.

[106]*Radikal*, April 23, 1998. Journalists attacked included Mert İlkutluğ of Milliyet, and Ahmet Şık and the columnist Celal Başlangıç of *Radikal*. İlkutluğ and Şık were knocked unconscious.

[107]Ibid.

[108]"Polise 3. soruşturma," *Milliyet* (Internet Edition), April 24, 1998.

crowd. Instead, the full fury was turned on the media....four camera men were injured seriously enough to require hospitalization.[109]

A reporter for a mainstream daily who covered similar Islamist demonstrations in August and September 1997 commented that,

> At Islamist demonstrations, both the demonstrators beat us up and the police beat us up....Last Friday, there was an attack on journalists at a Friday mosque demonstration. Some of the journalists caught one of the attackers and gave him to the police, who then sent him away. They never even detained him....We see this double standard toward Islamists. We don't, of course, want violence used against them, but they use violence against us and nothing happens. Yesterday, the Islamists had a protest in Beyazit. Nothing happened. Compare that with what happens with leftist students, who are beaten and tortured. A police official, Mehmet Cağlar, even shouted to the protestors, "Eh, Cemaat, we don't want to hurt you." At another incident, one policeman was shouting, "Don't illegalize your action." But the entire action was illegal as the demonstrators had not been given permission. Last Friday, the same policeman said to the press, "You are agitating the crowd. Leave."[110]

Police who attacked journalists during these demonstrations admitted that they had done so because "they were seeking revenge for having been presented in a bad light."[111]

During May Day demonstrations in 1998, supporters of the far-right Nationalist Action Party (*MHP*) hung a high school student—presumably a leftist—out of the window of their local headquarters and beat him viciously.[112] The MHP activists then attacked journalists covering the event. When they went

---

[109]"Can Turkey's Divisions be Healed," *Briefing* (Ankara), No. 1153, August 4, 1997, p. 3. Officials conducted an investigation into these incidents and met with press officials to work toward protecting the press during demonstrations, but little was achieved.

[110]The journalist requested anonymity. Interview, Istanbul, September 1997.

[111]*Briefing*, August 4, 1997, p. 3.

[112]"MHP binasında işkence," ("Torture in the MHP Building"), *Cumhuriyet Hafta*, May 8, 1998, p. 6.

to the nearest police station to complain, they were told that the man being beaten and hung out the window "was a fellow Grey Wolf (MHP activist) who was being restrained from leaping onto passing leftists."[113]

---

[113]"Grey Wolves, Police Beat Turkish Protester," Reuters, May 1, 1998. If the police version were true, the man's assault would have been a kamikaze attack as he was being hung from a three-story window.

VII. IMPRISONED JOURNALISTS

While no one—including the government—refutes the fact that journalists are imprisoned in Turkey on free expression charges, there is little consensus on the exact number. According to the U.S.-based Committee to Protect Journalists (CPJ), as of March 1998 there were twenty-nine journalists in jail on free expression charges.[114] Another thirteen journalists, according to the group, were imprisoned but their confinement could not be confirmed as being "directly related to their work."[115] On May 6, 1998, Reporters San Frontieres (RSF) called for the immediate release of two journalists imprisoned in Turkey.[116] In May 1997, RSF had announced that there were eight journalists in prison on free expression charges, but most of these were released after a limited August 1997 amnesty for imprisoned journalists.[117] At that time, the RSF General Secretariat and the RSF Istanbul Bureau stated that they could not establish whether seventy-seven other imprisoned press people (basın çalışan) were imprisoned because of "press crimes."[118] They promised, however, to investigate the issue. The Press Council of Turkey, which in the past had worked with CPJ, announced that there were eleven journalists in jail in Turkey as of March 31, 1998.[119] For its part, The Human Rights Foundation of Turkey lists sixty imprisoned journalists as of March 1998.[120]

It is difficult to arrive at a definitive number accepted by all because the overwhelming majority of journalists imprisoned in Turkey are ostensibly convicted not on press charges, but under either Article 168 of the penal code (membership in an armed group) or Article 169 (aiding an armed group).They

---

[114]Committee to Protect Journalists, *Attacks on the Press in 1997*, March 1998, p. 53.

[115]*Attacks on the Press 1997*, p. 72.

[116]The Reporters San Frontieres Newsletter, May 1998, No. 27, p. 5.

[117] RSF, *Türkiye Kayıp Düşler (Turkey: Lost Hopes)*, May 1997. The RSF representative in Turkey is Nadire Mater, who also serves as the Turkey bureau chief for the IPS news service. The drop in the RSF figure is the result of the August 1997 law suspending sentences for responsible editors.

[118]Ibid.

[119]"Press Council Says 11 Journalists Behind Bars," Reuters, March 31, 1998. Nail Güreli, the head of the Press Council, stated that, "We would like to underline our view that there is nothing to boast about in Turkey having 11 journalists in jail...But the truth is that Turkey is not the country with the highest number of journalists in prison."

[120]*Türkiye'de Basın Özgürlüğü*, pp. 52-58.

overwhelmingly write for publications sympathetic to armed groups. [121] Sometimes, these newspapers or magazines glorify acts of violence committed by the armed group with which the publication sympathizes.

Human Rights Watch believes that the mere act of working at a publication that sympathizes with an armed group is neither proof of membership in that group nor is it illegal in and of itself unless the individual in question writes articles openly calling for acts of violence and there is reason to believe that violence will result. Such utterances may not be protected speech under restrictions allowed under Article 10.2 of the European Convention for the Protection of Human Rights and Fundamental Freedoms, to which Turkey is a party.[122] Human Rights Watch is also concerned that individuals who work for such publications face serious police abuse and torture during interrogation and may not receive due process during their trials.

---

[121] *Kurtuluş* and *Mücadele*, for example, have an editorial policy sympathetic to Dev-Sol, an armed urban group that has carried out assassinations of retired army officers, police, and former government members. *Atılım* is believed sympathetic to the far-left Marxist-Leninist Communist Party (MLKP), which has conducted acts of violence. *Alınteri* is regarded as sympathetic to the Turkish Revolutionary Communist Union (TİKB), an urban guerilla group. Özgür Halk sympathizes with the PKK. All these groups are outlawed in Turkey. See Committee to Protect Journalists, *Attacks on the Press in 1997*, pp. 53-68.

[122]Article 10.1 grants the right of freedom of expression, while Article 10.2 outlines cases where the state may legally restrict that right. While the European Court of Human Rights has largely ruled against Turkey in cases involving torture and forced village evacuations, it recently ruled in its favor in a case concerning Article 10. The court ruled that Turkey had violated the rights of Mehdi Zana, the former mayor of Diyarbakır and a Kurdish political activist, regarding the right to a fair trial and length of detention, but it rejected Zana's allegation that his right to speech had been violated. Mr. Zana had made statements supporting the armed struggle of the PKK. See European Court of Human Rights, Case of Zana v. Turkey, No. 69/1996/688/880, Judgement, Strasbourg, November 25, 1997 and "Zana'ya ret, Türkiye Ceza," ("Rejection for Zana, Punishment for Turkey"), *Cumhuriyet Hafta*, November 28, 1997, p. 16. For further discussion of the European Court of Human Rights interpretation of restrictions of Article 10, see section, "INTERNATIONAL LEGAL OBLIGATIONS."

VIII. RESTRICTIONS ON FREE EXPRESSION

Arbitrariness

A capricious arbitrariness characterizes the punishment of free expression. This arbitrariness reflects the general political atmosphere during any given period. A journalist writes an article on a controversial topic without incident. A year later, however, the same reporter writing a similar story faces criminal charges. A series of articles may be published in a newspaper uneventfully, only to confront a legal challenge when republished as a book. A cartoonist for the satirical left-leaning political comic book *Leman* commented that, "One year it is okay, nothing happens. It seems as if they don't follow you. Then all of a sudden the authorities start to make a fuss over nothing."[123] Mustafa Islamoğlu, an Islamic intellectual, commented that, "There is a space that does exist. It was not given, but taken by force. There is no general tendency. It is not unidirectional. It is a hit-and-run type thing. Sometimes the oppressing forces attack and try to push away the alternative forces and vice-versa."[124] Ahmet Altan, a leading columnist and novelist, observed that,

> You can say there is no freedom of expression, you can say there is press freedom, and you are right in both statements. It's not like in a typical dictatorship—the borders are not clear, you can't know where they are. The application of the law is arbitrary. But in many ways the arbitrariness is worse. You don't know when you will get into trouble.[125]

Turkey's antiquated legal framework provides a basis for arbitrary actions. Though amended numerous times, the Turkish Penal Code dates from 1926, when

---

[123]Interview with Metin Üstündağ, cartoonist for the weekly *Leman*, Istanbul, Turkey, August 1997. As of August 1997, sixty-eight out of the 300 issues of *Leman* published to date were met with some type of criminal action from state authorities.

[124]Interview, Istanbul, August 1997. In 1995-1996, Mr. Islamoğlu was imprisoned for one year on free expression charges for violating *The Law Concerning Crimes Committed Against Atatürk/ Atatürk Aleyhine İşlenen Suçlar Hakkında Kanun* (No. 5816).

[125]Interview with Ahmet Altan, novelist and columnist for *Yeni Yüzyıl*, an Istanbul daily, August 1997.

it was adopted from Mussolini's Italy.[126] During that period, according to Bernard Lewis, a leading scholar on Turkey, "Political activity against the regime was banned and newspapers were under strict control."[127] Another scholar, Kemal Karpat, has written that, "The press was most tightly controlled, both in its daily work and in obtaining permission for founding new publications. A *Basın Birliği* (Press Union) was instituted for controlling the press."[128]

In 1946, however, after twenty-three years of virtually unchallenged, authoritarian one-party rule, the Republican People's Party (CHP) agreed to the introduction of a multi-party system. As part of the transition, martial law was lifted in 1947 and liberalizations were introduced at universities and in the electoral and association laws.[129] Furthermore, the Press Law was liberalized, a partial press amnesty was introduced, and the executive lost the power to close newspapers, which reverted to the courts.[130] After a crushing defeat in the 1950 elections, the CHP peacefully handed power to the newly-founded Democrat Party.

Even after this peaceful transition to multi-party democracy, however, much of the restrictive legal framework of the penal code was left intact. In fact, new laws restricting free expression were passed, some directed against Islamists and some at communists.[131] One scholar has argued that,

> By definition, a transition to democracy necessitates an increase
> in freedoms; in Turkey, however, changes in the penal code at

---

[126]The Turkish Criminal Code, adopted in 1926, is based on the Italian Criminal Code of 1889. It has been amended on many occasions, and to date approximately half of the articles have been changed. See, Tuğrul Ansay and Don Wallace, Jr., eds, *Introduction to Turkish Law* (The Hague: Kluwer Law International, 1996), pp. 163-174.

Sometimes the amendment had made the penal code article more severe, as with the 1981 amendment to Article 312. See section, "Domestic Law."

[127]Bernard Lewis, *The Emergence of Modern Turkey* (London: Oxford University Press, 1968), p. 304. Lewis, adds, however, that, "...Apart from this, talk, and even books and periodicals, were comparatively free."

[128]Kemal H. Karpat, *Turkey's Politics: The Transition to a Multi-Party System* (Princeton: Princeton University Press, 1959), p. 74.

[129]Ahmad, p. 106; Lewis, p. 309; Karpat, pp. 158-9.

[130]Karpat, pp. 158-9.

[131]For example, a law to penalize anyone who "insults or curses the memory of Atatürk was passed in 1951. See section, Domestic Law, *The Law Concerning Crimes Committed Against Atatürk/ Atatürk Aleyhine İşlenen Suçlar Hakkında Kanun* (No. 5816, adopted July 25, 1951).

the time of this transition increased penalties for already outlawed acts like left-wing propaganda and organization.[132]

Further reform was often counterbalanced by new steps backward. Many of the freedoms granted in the 1961 constitution, considered an extremely liberal and enlightened document, were rescinded by Law No. 1488, passed in September 1971 by a technocratic government installed by the military in the wake of the "Coup by Memorandum" of March 12, 1971.[133] The 1982 constitution, passed after the military coup of September 12, 1980, further regressed from the rights granted in the constitution of 1961 and codified many of the restrictions of Law No. 1488.

Although numerous draconian laws exist on the books, the scope of what can be discussed without fear of prosecution has grown to include most topics. Even when cases are opened, people still speak their minds. Oral Çalışlar, a columnist with the Istanbul daily *Cumhuriyet*, commented that after he received a two-year sentence under Article 8 of the Anti-Terror Law, Murat Karayalçın, then chairman of the Social Democratic People's Party (SHP), the junior partner in the coalition government at the time, called him to consult about amending the very law under which Mr. Çalışlar had been convicted.[134] He added that, "It was hard for two Canadian journalists I know to understand this. For example, the fact that I was working for state television and I received a sentence for separatist propaganda." In one of his columns, he quipped that,

> Watching Yaşar Kemal on the television program Siyaset Meydanı, I started to say to myself: Turkey is a strange country of contradictions. Our famous writer, one of Turkey's outstanding people, has become the topic of one its most

---

[132]See Taner Timur's essay, "The Ottoman Heritage," in Irvin C. Schick and Ertuğrul Ahmet Tonak, eds, *Turkey in Transition: New Perspectives* (New York & Oxford: Oxford University Press, 1987), p. 18.

[133]*Constitution of the Turkish Republic*, translated for the Committee of National Unity by Sadık Balkan, Ahmet E. Uysal, and Kemal H. Karpat. Ankara, 1961; Kanun (Law) No. 1488, passed on September 20, 1971. Published in the Official Gazette, No. 13964, on October 22, 1971.

[134]Article 8 was amended in October 1995. Mr. Çalişlar's sentence was overturned. He was retried for the same case; the verdict is still pending.

important programs. For hours he is defending the ideas for which he was convicted.[135]

Erbil Tüşalp, a columnist for the Istanbul daily *Radikal,* had a case opened against him for insulting then minister of justice, Şevket Kazan. According to Tüşalp, "I wrote that in a government with such people, I am ashamed to be a citizen. I guess Şevket Kazan took it personally. When I learned that I was going to be tried, I wrote another article saying that 'We would meet.'"[136]

A host of laws exist that can be employed when the state feels threatened or wishes to target certain individuals. A study on the Kurdish conflict has noted, for example, that, "There is almost an indirect relationship between the level of PKK activities and the ability of columnists, as well as others, to discuss non-military solutions to the Kurdish question. The best example came about during the cease-fire of 1993, when newspapers were full of stories about the PKK, which—while mostly negative—did not exhibit the hard edge they usually do."[137] Mr. Çalişlar, the *Cumhuriyet* columnist, commented that,

> When state wants to take steps for democracy there becomes a bit more freedom. Four years earlier, during the period of the cease-fire, you could discuss all, including a peaceful solution. When the cease-fire ended...if you talked about such topics, you could get into trouble.[138]

As in many criminal justice systems throughout the world, penalties in Turkey vary according to the social status of the violator. Without exception, most individuals whom Human Rights Watch interviewed stated that newspaper

---

[135]Oral Çalışlar, "Çelişmeler Ülkesi Türkiye," ("Turkey, the Land of Contradictions"), *Cumhuriyet*, October 28, 1996. In 1996, Mr. Kemal was convicted and given a suspended sentence under Article 312 for two articles he wrote that appeared in the book, *Düşünce Özgürlüğü ve Türkiye (Freedom of Thought and Turkey).* Siyaset Meydani is a popular political talk show.

[136]Interview, Ankara, August 1997. Tüşalp was acquitted in March 1998.

[137]Barkey and Fuller, p. 122.

[138]Interview, Istanbul, August 1997. The PKK declared a unilateral cease-fire in 1993. Although the state did not officially recognize the offer, there appeared to be a reduction in fighting and an easing of tension in southeastern Turkey, the main region of the conflict. The PKK ended its cease-fire in May 1993 when, after stopping a bus near Bingöl, it murdered thirty-three recently demobilized and unarmed soldiers and five civilians.

columnists in the mainstream press—many of whom enjoy near superstar status—have the most freedom to write as they please. Ahmet Altan, the novelist and *Yeni Yüzyıl* columnist, observed that, "I am not a good example. I write a critical article, it is printed. I'm older. I get into trouble, I get even more fame... If someone writes the same thing, it might not happen."[139] Oral Çalişlar, the *Cumhuriyet* columnist, put himself in the same category with Mr. Altan: "I am one of the people who has the fewest limits. Even though I am not afraid of violating them, it is a factor."[140]

If criminal proceedings are brought against such writers, they are almost never detained and their cases usually end in acquittal or suspended sentences.[141] Ali Bayramoğlu, a former professor and columnist with *Yeni Yüzyıl* added that, "It depends on who you are if they effect you directly or indirectly. My identity saves me, and my cases often end in acquittal....[In one case] I should have been guilty [according to the law]. But I was acquitted."[142]

Those writing for Kurdish nationalist newspapers and for radical left-wing publications occupy the bottom rung of the hierarchy, and a large number of cases are opened against them.[143] These publications are sometimes closed by state authorities, either temporarily or permanently—a punishment that rarely strikes mainstream newspapers. Yurduşun Özsökmenter, assistant general publishing coordinator for the Kurdish nationalist paper *[Ülkede] Gündem* stated that, "We started the paper in July 1997. Since then twenty of the forty-one issues we have printed have been confiscated....In addition, almost every day one of our distributors has been harassed."[144] When cases are opened, the indicted are often remanded into custody and sometimes face mistreatment and torture during police interrogation. Prosecutions often end in conviction.

The following three cases represent both the arbitrary and hierarchical application of laws limiting freedom of expression. In two of the cases, journalists were prosecuted for writing an article despite the fact that they had written similar

---

[139]Interview, Istanbul, August 1997.

[140]Interview, Istanbul, August 1997.

[141]There is no bail system in Turkey. If one is charged, the prosecutor can demand that the suspect be remanded into custody during the trial (*tutuklu*) or be allowed to remain free (*tutuksuz*).

[142]Interview, Istanbul, November 1997.

[143]Such publications often have editorial policies sympathetic to armed groups, such as the PKK or Dev-Sol.

[144]Interview, Istanbul, August 1997. Figure as of August 1997.

stories at an earlier date without charge. In the third case, three journalists were prosecuted for writing about a topic on which others reported without incident.

A respected journalist who has worked for the BBC, AFP, the French daily *Libération*, as well as a number of Turkish publications, Ragip Duran interviewed the leader of the PKK, Abdullah Öcalan, twice, once in 1991 and again in 1994. In March 1991, Mr. Duran published articles based on the interview in the center-left Istanbul daily *Cumhuriyet*.[145] No prosecution followed. A little over three years later, Mr. Duran again interviewed the PKK leader. This time, however, he published his article in the now-closed, Kurdish nationalist daily *Özgür Gündem*.[146] Mr. Duran and a colleague were subsequently charged under Article 7.2 of the Anti-Terror Law, which prohibits conducting propaganda for illegal organizations.[147] While a lower court found his colleague innocent, Mr. Duran was sentenced to ten months of imprisonment and a fine of TL333,333,333 (around U.S. $4,000 at the time).[148] He is currently serving his prison term at Saray prison outside Istanbul.

Timing clearly played a role in the prosecution of Mr. Duran. In early 1991, when he interviewed the PKK leader the first time, then President Özal was pushing for increased rights for Turkey's Kurds.[149] During the general elections of October 1991, then leader of the True Path Party (DYP) Süleyman Demirel,

---

[145]See "Apo'dan 3 Mesaj" ("Three Messages from Apo"), *Cumhuriyet*, Istanbul, March 23, 1991; "Şam'da bir Kürt Zapata'sı" ("A Kurdish Zapata in Damascus"), *Cumhuriyet*, Istanbul, March 24, 1991; "Apo'dan Türkiye: Siyasi, askeri birliğe evet" ("From Apo to Turkey: Yes to a Political and Military Union"), *Cumhuriyet*, Istanbul, March 24, 1997.

[146]See Ragip Duran, "Apo91/Öcalan 94", *Özgür Gündem*, Istanbul, April 12, 1994.

[147]According to Article 7.2 of the Anti-Terror Law, "Those who assist members of organizations formed in the manner described above or who make propaganda in connection with such an organization—even if their offense constitutes a separate crime—are to be sentenced from one to five years and given a heavy fine from fifty to one hundred million lira."

[148]On October 23, 1997, the High Court of Appeals (*Yargıtay*), confirmed the sentence. In June 1998, Mr. Duran was remanded into custody and sent to prison. Under the Anti-Terror law, those sentenced under the Anti-Terror law must serve three quarters of their sentence.

[149]On April 11, 1991, under pressure from Mr. Özal, parliament repealed *The Law Concerning Publications in Languages Other than Turkish/Türkçeden Başka Dillerlerle Yapılacak Yayınlar Hakkında Kanun (No. 2932)*. For a chronology of the struggle to abolish the law, see Koray Düzgören, *Kürt Çıkmazı (The Kurdish Dead-end)*, (Istanbul: Vyayınları, 1994), pp. 74-6.

announced that Turkey had acknowledged a "Kurdish reality." That same month, then President Özal told the daily *Hürriyet* that, "We will solve the Kurdish issue. It will be the last service I will do for my country. We must discuss every topic openly, including a federation."[150] By 1994, however, when the second interview was published, fighting between security forces and the PKK was at its height.

Furthermore, while many liberal-left columnists and contributors contributed to *Özgür Gündem,* the paper's overall editorial line was largely viewed as sympathetic to the goals of the PKK.[151] *Cumhuriyet*, on the other hand, although often critical of shortcomings in Turkish democracy and the rule of law, is generally seen as a pro-Kemalist paper.

The second case involves Oral Çalişlar, a *Cumhuriyet* columnist. In early 1993, Mr. Çalişlar conducted a lengthy interview with Mr. Öcalan and with Kemal Burkay, the head of the Socialist Party of Kurdistan (SPK). The interview ran for eighteen days as a series of full-page articles in *Cumhuriyet.* No criminal proceedings were opened against him or the paper. Mr. Çalişlar even joked that a public prosecutor called him to congratulate him on the interview:

> Let me explain something comical to you. The head public prosecutor then, Ahmet Kőksal, called me and said, "It was a great interview. Good job." He was talking about the interview I did with Öcalan and Burkay, which ran as a series in Cumhuriyet in 1993. There was a preliminary investigation, but it was dropped, absolutely no problem.[152]

When the series of interviews was published in book form in September 1993, however, the State Security Court in Istanbul banned the publication under Article 28 of the constitution, deeming it to be "separatist propaganda."[153] Shortly

---

[150]See Düzgören, p. 110. Mr Demirel became prime minister after the elections.

[151]Mr. Öcalan, for example, wrote a column in the paper under the byline of "Ali Fırat," or "Ali Euphrates."

[152]Interview, Istanbul, August, 1997. The prosecutor issued a so-called *takipsizlik* decision, which means that there are no grounds for legal action.

[153]Oral Çalişlar, *Öcalan ve Burkay'la Kürt Sorunu* (*The Kurdish Question with Öcalan and Burkay*), (Istanbul: Pencere Yayınları, September 1993).

Müteferrik Karar (Banning Decision), No. 1993/297, Istanbul State Security Court No. 3, November 5, 1993. Article 28 of the constitution states that,

Anyone who writes or prints any news or articles threatening the internal or

thereafter, Mr. Çalişlar and the book's publisher, Muzaffer Erdoğan, were charged under Articles 8.1 and 8.2 for conducting separatist propaganda.[154] The indictment stated that, "It is understood that separatist propaganda has been made by stating that one part of the land of the State of the Republic of Turkey was shown as Kurdistan, that the Kurdish people are a separate nation, and are fighting a war of national liberation..."[155] In October 1994, both men were found guilty: Mr. Çalişlar was fined and given a two-year sentence; Mr. Erdoğan was given six months and fined.[156] When Article 8 was amended in October 1995, the sentences were reduced, but the state prosecutor appealed to restore the original penalties. The case is being retried.

Again, timing played a role. The interview appeared during a cease-fire, which, although not officially recognized by state authorities, held for nearly two months. The banning of the book and the subsequent prosecution occurred during an escalation of the conflict.[157]

---

external security of the state or the indivisible integrity of the state with its territory and nation, which tend to incite offense, riot or insurrection, or which refer to classified state secrets and anyone who prints or transmits such news or articles to others for the above purpose shall be held responsible under the law relevant to these offenses....

[154]Istanbul State Security Court No. 1, Iddianame (Indictment) No. 1993/1061, November 26, 1993. Both men were tried without being remanded into custody.

[155]Ibid.

[156]Istanbul State Security Court No. 1, Karar (Decision), No. 1994/237, October 27, 1994.

[157]The book was banned in November 1993. October 1993 witnessed unprecedented violence. Between October 20-23, security forces destroyed much of the district capital of Lice, Diyarbakır province, using disproportionate force following a small clash with the PKK. Approximately 640 homes and businesses were damaged, and at least thirty people died, most of them civilians. The use of such disproportionate force may have been retaliation for the death of Diyarbakır Gendarmerie Regional Commander Brigadier General Bahtiyar Aydın, who was shot and killed in Lice on October 22, 1993. In addition, there were sixty-nine so-called "unknown actor" (*faili meçhul*) death squad killings in October 1993. Many believe such attacks were carried out by shadowy groups linked to security forces or with the connivance of state authorities.

For its part, the PKK in October 1993 murdered at least 123 civilians, including thirty-eight in one reprisal attack against a town in the Çat district of Erzurum in retaliation for the violence in Lice. On October 24, President Demirel stated that, "If these events go on like this, martial law can come on the agenda." See Duzgören, pp. 450-462; Human Rights Foundation of Turkey, *1993 Turkey Human Rights Report* (Ankara, Turkey, June 1994), pp. 61-64 and 77-80; Ismet G. Imset, "Fighting Separatist Terrorism," *Turkish Probe* (Ankara), November 4, 1993, pp. 4-6.

The third case involves three journalists who were prosecuted for interviewing two former PKK members, Murat Ipek and Murat Demir. Ahmet Sümbül and Zeynal Bağır of the now-banned Kurdish nationalist *Demokrasi* newspaper and Abdulkadir Konuksever of the mainstream ATV television station were remanded into custody in the summer of 1997 and charged under Article 169, aiding and abetting the PKK.[158] According to the indictment, "The suspects...acting according to the goals of the illegal PKK terror organization, by use of pressure and threat forced Murat Ipek and Murat Demir to make statements to the press and in television, and thus helped the PKK organization."[159] In articles that appeared in *Demokrasi*, Mr. Ipek and Mr. Demir alleged that they committed in conjunction with security forces several death squad style murders, including those of the ethnic Kurdish poet Musa Anter.[160]

The two men, however, had previously made similar statements to two prominent journalists and appeared before a Turkish parliamentary commission investigating the January 1993 car-bomb murder of investigative journalist Uğur Mumcu. According to the Yaşar Altürk, counsel to the three accused:

> Murat Ipek and Murat Demir said the same things to my clients as they did to numerous other journalists. They [the two former PKK members] spoke to the Uğur Mumcu Investigation Commission in parliament. They spoke to Mehmet Ali Birand of the program "32nd Day." They spoke to Kadir Çelik of the "Objektif" program on Show TV. The prosecution says that my clients forced Ipek and Demir to speak and say these things in line with orders from the PKK. But there is absolutely no evidence for this. If what Murat Ipek had stated occurred only in Diyarbakır, maybe one could believe such an allegation. But he said these things all over Turkey and to many journalists and others as well.[161]

---

[158]Diyarbakır State Security Court Iddianame (Indictment), No. 1997/933, August 6, 1997. Messr. Sümbül and Konuksever were remanded into custody June 4, 1997; Miss Bağır, on July 24, 1997.

[159]Ibid.

[160]"Anter'i biz öldürdük" ("We Killed Anter"), *Demokrasi,* Istanbul, February 10, 1997; "Hantepe katliamı itirafı" ("Hantepe Massacre Confession"), *Demokrasi,* February 11, 1997.

[161]Interview, Diyarbakır, August 1997.

On October 6, 1997, Messrs. Sümbül and Konuksever and Ms. Bağır were released from custody, though their trial continued until September 22, 1998, when they were acquitted.

Prosecution and Repression of the Kurdish-Nationalist Press and Writers

Ethnic Kurds who express a group or political identity that is uniquely Kurdish face severe prosecution and repression from the state.[162] "Pro-Kurdish" or "nationalist Kurdish" publications and writers run a fairly broad ideological gamut. Some have an editorial policy sympathetic to the PKK or openly support the PKK. The head of the PKK, Abdullah Öcalan, even used to write a column under the pen name "Ali Euphrates" in one of the Kurdish-nationalist dailies, *Özgür Gündem*. Other Kurdish-nationalist publications support one of the smaller legal political parties or parties that, while not engaged in violence, remain outlawed in Turkey, such as Kemal Burkay's Socialist Party of Kurdistan (SPK).

All these newspapers, however, share one thing in common: they all face serious abuses, such as the assassination of journalists by shadowy death squads, imprisonment, mistreatment while in police detention, and the confiscation and closing of newspapers. When cases are opened against those working at Kurdish-nationalist publications, the incidence of guilty verdicts and of remand into custody appears to be higher than with prosecutions involving mainstream journalists.[163] Such cases usually, though not exclusively, involve prosecution under Article 312.2 of the penal code and Article 8 of the Anti-Terror Law. The following cases, while not exhaustive, are illustrative of such prosecutions.

•   In June 1997, Ahmet Zeki Okçuoğlu, a lawyer and owner of the Doz publishing house, entered prison to serve a ten-month sentence for his

---

[162]There is no accurate term, either in Turkish or in English, to describe such individuals. For lack of a better term they are often referred to as "pro-Kurdish" or "Kurdish-nationalist." More precisely, this means that they are unhappy with the officially monoethnic Kemalist state and want some type of legal anchoring of their Kurdish identity. This could run from minority language and cultural rights to autonomy.

Some ethnic Kurds, however, have made peace with the Kemalist state and do not seek a unique, legal recognition of their identity. All political parties, for example, have ethnic Kurdish deputies in parliament. Furthermore, intermarriage between Sunni Turks and Sunni Kurds is widespread.

[163]This is probably due not to ethnicity, but to the fact that prosecutors and courts often view the publications for which they write as radical and thus a greater threat to public order.

1995 conviction under Article 159 of the penal code.[164] Mr. Okçuoğlu, along with his responsible editor, Sedat Karakaş, were charged with "insulting the moral identity of the Republic and Judiciary" for an article Mr. Okçuoğlu wrote for the bilingual, Turkish-Kurdish weekly *Azadi* (*Freedom*).[165] The court ruled that, "In the article titled, 'The Turkish Republic Does Not Want to Make Peace with the Kurds,' which is the subject of the trial and was written by Ahmet Zeki Okçuoğlu, the moral personality of the Turkish Republic was insulted [by stating that] the Turkish Republic took the Kurds under control by force, denied their identity and national rights, conducted genocide against Kurds, worked to assimilate them, denied the existence of Kurds, by illegal methods took their rights, and, furthermore, qualified the Turkish Republic as terrorist..."[166]

• Yılmaz Odabaşı, a writer and journalist who has worked at various newspapers, faced three separate prosecutions connected with his book, *Düş ve Yaşam (Hope and Life)*. Two were directly because of the work and one was related to a statement he made during a court hearing. The three cases included one under Article 8 of the Anti-Terror Law for "separatist" propaganda; a second under both Law No. 5816 for insulting "Atatürk," the founder of the Turkish republic and under Article 145 of the penal code for insulting the flag or other "symbols of state sovereignty"; and a third case under Article 159 for "insulting the court."[167]

---

[164]Information on Mr. Okçuoğlu came from a September 1997 interview with his brother, Selim Okçuoğlu, as well as from documents provided.

[165]T.C. Istanbul 2. Ağır Ceza Mahkemesi, Karar 1995/4, January 19, 1995. The article was titled, "The Turkish Republic Does Not Want to Make Peace with the Kurds," ("T.C. Kürtler'le barışmak istemiyor), *Azadi*, April 11-17, 1993.

Azadi was forced to close under state pressure in 1993. It is now published as *Hêvi (Hope)*, which has an editorial policy sympathetic to the Socialist Party of Kurdistan of Kemal Burkay.

[166]T.C. Istanbul 2. Ağır Ceza Mahkemesi, Karar 1995/4, ibid.

[167] The book is a collection of his articles that appeared in the weekly *Aydınlık* and in the newspaper *Siyah Beyaz*. His publisher, Niyazi Koçak, was charged in the first two cases as well. Unless otherwise noted information comes from an interview with Mr. Odabaşı, Ankara, September 1997.

In the first case, Mr. Odabaşı was sentenced to eighteen months of imprisonment and a fine of TL933 million (U.S. $7594) in March 1997, while his publisher was given a fine of TL67.85 million (U.S. $522) under Article 8 of the Anti-Terror Law. In the indictment, the prosecutor charged that,

> Having examined the contents of the book in question, it has been indicated that in Turkey—despite the existence of the Turkish people—there is another people with a perspective based on race, and that the struggle against the illegal separatist terror organization is actually a struggle of a people for their identity by stating that these people moan under state terror.[168]

For his part, Mr. Odabaşı stated that, "I am not a supporter of the idea of an independent Kurdish state. However, in our country the existence of Kurds also cannot be denied. If mentioning the existence of Kurds is separatism, then I am a separatist."[169] The case is presently on appeal.

In the second case, Mr. Odabaşi and his publisher, Niyazi Koçak, were acquitted on appeal of charges of "insulting Atatürk" and "insulting the national anthem" in April 1998. In overturning the two-year and six-month sentence, the High Appeals Court (*Yargıtay*) ruled that, "The thoughts that Yılmaz Odabaşı expressed and wrote remained within the borders of criticism." In the indictment, the prosecutor had argued that the following statement had "insulted the memory of Atatürk:"

> Didn't Kemalism slaughter Mustafa Suphi and his comrades? Didn't Kemalism throw Nazım in jail for years because he was a communist? In the southeast, from Dersim to the Sheik Said rebellions, weren't hundreds of villages burned and tens of thousands slaughtered in the most frightening way under the directives of Mustafa Kemal and then under the special auspices of Fetih Okyar and others.[170]

---

[168]T.C. Ankara Devlet Güvenlik Mahkemesi, İddianame (Indictment) No. 1996/106, October 10, 1996.

[169]"Şair Yazar Yılmaz Odabaşı yargılandı," (The Poet-writer Yılmaz Odabaşı is on Trial) *Cumhuriyet,* November 20, 1996.

[170]Press Office, Republic of Turkey, State Prosecutor's Office, Indictment No. 1996/167, November 20, 1996.

Finally, upon the announcement of the sentence in the first case in March 1997, Mr. Odabaşı exclaimed to the chief judge of the State Security Court, "I am ashamed to live in the same country as you." For this he was remanded into custody and charged with "insulting the court." He was quickly released from detention, but on September 14, 1998, Mr. Odabaşı was sentenced to seven months in this trial.

- In August 1996, Fatih Yeşilbağ, who served as the responsible editor of the now-closed pro-Kurdish daily *Özgür Gündem* during the period between August and September 1993, was remanded into custody and put on trial under Article 159 of the penal code and Article 8 of the Anti-Terror Law. He was released from prison after Law No. 4304 was passed in August 1997, which suspended the sentences and cases of responsible editors.[171]

Prosecution and Pressure on the Islamist Press

Pressure against the Islamist press, writers and others has increased markedly over the past two years, a result of the Turkish military's fear of what it perceives as the increasing Islamization of society.[172] Turkey has a broad spectrum of Islamist publications, ranging from independent to pro-Iranian. Major Islamist dailies include *Zaman, Yeni Şafak, Akit, and Milli Gazete. Zaman* is a mass-circulation, quality daily published by a holding company associated with Fetullah Gülen, a moderate who preaches a Turkish-Islamic synthesis. *Yeni Şafak* is considered a paper for Islamist intellectuals, while *Milli Gazete* supports the now-banned Welfare Party and its successor, Fazilet. *Akit* is considered the most radical of the lot. Islamist television stations include Samanyolu and Channel 7, among others.

Two main laws are primarily used to prosecute Islamists. The first, Law No. 5816, "concerning crimes committed against Atatürk," penalizes anyone who

---

[171]Law No. 4304, "The Law Concerning Suspension of Trials Opened Against and Penalties Given to Responsible Editors," resulted in the mandatory release from prison of a total of eight individuals, including another *Özgür Gündem* editor, Işık Yurtçu. All eight received three-year suspended sentences.

[172]The Islamist government of Necmettin Erbakan—formed in June 1996— was forced from power in June 1997 thanks to a military-sponsored campaign. Mr. Erbakan's Welfare Party was closed in February 1998. For more on the military, *see*, "The Role of the Military."

"publicly insults or curses the memory of Atatürk."[173] As the number of prosecutions has risen, however, state authorities increasingly use Article 312.2 of the penal code which prohibits, "openly incit[ing] people to enmity and hatred by pointing to class, racial, religious, confessional, or regional differences..." There has even been the suggestion of reinstituting Article 163 of the penal code which was used in the past to penalize Islamists and was abolished in 1991 after the passage of the Anti-Terror Law.[174] Before its abolition, Article 163.4 punished those who, "contrary to secularism, make propaganda or suggestions with the purpose of adopting, even partially, the basic social, economic, political, or judicial structures of the State based on religious principles or beliefs or with the purpose of obtaining political benefits or personal influence by making use of religion or religious sentiments or sacred things...."

The following cases are representative of prosecutions against Islamist politicians, intellectuals, and writers.

- On April 22, 1998, the popular mayor of greater Istanbul, Recep Tayyip Erdoğan of the Islamist Fazilet Party, the successor of the now-banned Welfare Party, was sentenced to ten months of imprisonment under Article 312.2 of the penal code and fined TL716,666 (U.S. $14.58). Mr. Erdoğan was prosecuted for a speech he made in Siirt in December 1997 in which he quoted the following poem: "The minarets are our swords, the mosques are barracks, the domes are helmets."[175] The poem, which served as the basis for the prosecution, was written by Ziya Gökalp, an ethnic Kurd who is considered the intellectual father of Turkish nationalism. Initially, the Diyarbakır State Security Court prosecutor, who has jurisdiction for Siirt, decided not to prosecute the case.[176] In September 1998, the High Court of Appeals (*Yargıtay*) confirmed the conviction. Mr.

---

[173]*Atatürk Aleyhine İşlenen Suçlar Hakkında Kanun* (No. 5816, adopted July 25, 1951). The law states that, "Anyone who publicly insults or curses the memory of Atatürk shall be imprisoned with a heavy sentence of between one and three years....If the crimes outlined in the first article are committed by a group of two or more individuals, or publicly, or in public districts or by means of the press, they will have the penalty imposed increased by a proportion of one-half."

[174]"Turkey Plans Military-Inspired, Anti-Islamist Law," Reuters, January 28, 1998.

[175]"Erdoğan'a 10 ay hapis" ("Ten Months Imprisonment for Erdoğan"), *Cumhuriyet Hafta*, April 24, 1998.

[176] Kemal Çelik, "Erdoğan'a takipsizlik" ("Lack of Grounds for Legal Actions against Erdoğan"), *Milliyet* (Internet Edition), February 2, 1998.

Erdoğan—a favorite for reelection as mayor and possible successor as leader of the main Islamist party—is banned from politics for life under Turkish law because of the conviction.

- Mustafa İslamoğlu, an Islamist intellectual and writer, has been prosecuted several times and imprisoned twice because of his writings and speeches.[177] In October 1995, he was remanded into custody after his sentence under Article 159, "insulting Turkishness and the Republic," was confirmed upon appeal. Mr. İslamoğlu was prosecuted because of a speech in November 1993 at a forum on the Kurdish question organized by the Islamist human rights group, Mazlum-Der. The court ruled that,

> He gave a talk on the Kurdish question. In this talk, with an Islamist philosophical point of view, he criticized the period of the Ottoman Empire starting with Tanzimat together with the Republican period. He stated that in Anatolia unity cannot be achieved on the basis of racism. He stated that people of many races lived in Anatolia. Racism gave way to disunity. He stated that the common identity of those living in Turkey is Islam. Consequently, unity could be achieved in an Islamic framework. He stated that the heart of the slogan "How happy is he who calls himself Turk" was a slogan that smelled of an ignorant and rotting racism...As outlined in the details above, the individual who openly insulted and ridiculed the Republic...shall be punished according to penal code Article 159/1 to one year of heavy imprisonment...[178]

While he was in prison on the first charge, a second conviction under the "Law Concerning Crimes Committed Against Atatürk" was upheld by the High Court of Appeals. The prosecution stemmed from a December 13, 1993, article, "Black Voice" (*Kara Ses*) in the weekly *Selam*.[179] The

---

[177]Unless otherwise noted, information comes from an interview with Mustafa Islamoğlu, Istanbul, August 1997.

[178]Republic of Turkey, Heavy Penalty Court Number One, decision No. 1994/31, February 15, 1994.

[179]*Selam* has a pro-Iranian editorial policy.

prosecutor instituted the charges because Mr. İslamoğlu allegedly referred to the founder of the Republic of Turkey, Mustafa Kemal, as "a dictator." In his written defense, Mr. İslamoğlu's lawyer argued that,

> ....When my client's article is evaluated, it is seen that [my] client has dealt with the 270-year period of "Westernism and the Process of Westernization." A direct connection with Atatürk cannot be seen in the topic of the piece. In the writing the criticism is of the political movement that has the name Westernism and has its roots stretching from Ahmet III and Damad Ibrahim Paşa...the piece is a whole....The word "Dictator" mentioned has more to do with a party dictatorship, than with a person....Many documents have shown that the methods of administration of the Atatürk period could be qualified as a dictatorship, not a democracy. Even Atatürk himself personally established this determination. On July 23, 1930, he himself confessed to Fethi Okyar, one of the leading figures of the national struggle, that his administration was a dictatorship.[180]

Mr. İslamoğlu served a total of one year on both charges.

• On March 5, 1998, Aydın Koral, the general publications director of the weekly *Selam* was convicted of violating Article 312.2 of the penal code for a May 16, 1997, article, "Secular Militarist Oligarchy and Jerusalem Occupier Zionism." Mr. Koral, was given twenty months, though the case is on appeal. Under the press law, the court closed *Selam* for two weeks

---

[180] The defense makes reference to the memoirs of Fethi Okyar, *Üç Devirde bir Adam* (One Man in Three Epochs), published in 1980. Mustafa Kemal had asked Mr. Okyar to found an opposition party. Authorities, however, quickly closed the party Mr. Okyar founded, the Free Republican Party, shortly after its opening in 1930.

because of the conviction.[181] Koral's article spoke of the danger of increasing ties between Israel and Turkey.[182]

Prosecution of the Mainstream Press and Writers

Although the mainstream press has the greatest latitude to debate sensitive issues, it too faces state censure. Those prosecuted are usually columnists or other high-ranking journalists who have the authority to write as they please—and thus the capacity to violate taboos. Copy of low-level journalists, on the other hand, usually is filtered through editors, who often tone down or eliminate "problematic reporting."[183] Mainstream journalists who are charged are rarely detained during their trial. Often they are acquitted or given suspended sentences, as if the members of the court feel unease at condemning individuals whom they most likely read and, possibly, admire. At times, however, even mainstream journalists are imprisoned. At present, this is the exception, rather than the rule. The following four cases are illustrative of such prosecutions.

- On June 16, 1998, Umur Talu, a columnist for the Istanbul daily *Milliyet*, reporter Zeliha Midilli, and their responsible editor, Eren Güvener, were acquitted on charges of "insulting the court" (penal code Article 159) for critical articles and columns about the "Manisa trial."[184] In a column titled, "Torture, Truncheon, and Pocket Telephone," Mr. Talu complained that those on trial were found guilty despite the fact that little evidence of the crime existed apart from testimony allegedly taken under torture.[185] He

---

[181]TİHV, *Türkiye'de Basın Özgürlüğü (Press Freedom in Turkey)*, March 1998, p. 12. *See also* section, "The Confiscation of Publications and Books and the Closing of Newspapers." In a related case, Mr. Koral was sentenced to two years, commuted into a fine, for another article he wrote, and *Selam* was closed for one month.

[182]"Turkish Court Convicts Journalist," Associated Press, March 5, 1998.

[183]See section, "Self-Censorship."

[184]On January 15, 1997, ten individuals, most of them high-school students from Manisa, were found guilty of membership in an illegal organization despite serious allegations that incriminating statements they gave while in police detention were taken under torture. Those statements provided the basis of the state's case. Five others were acquitted in the case.

Article 159 punishes, "those who publicly insult or ridicule the moral personality of Turkishness, the Republic, the Parliament, the Government, State Ministers, the military or security forces of the state, or the Judiciary."

[185]Umur Talu, "Iskence, Cop, Cep,"("Torture, Truncheon, and Pocket Telephone,") *Milliyet (*Internet Edition), January 18, 1997.

commented that,"If the judiciary, in the trial of incident where torture has been proven, is not going to question the files submitted to the court, what is the use of hearings. Then, let the police stations give punishments. It's like that most of the time anyway, but what I mean is let's make it official and be done with it. So, this is what dependent judiciary is; in the sense of being dependent on torture." Ms. Midilli was charged for an article she wrote in the January 18, 1997, edition of *Milliyet*, "Bu karar çok tartışılacak" ("This Verdict is Really Debatable.")

• After being interviewed by Nilgün Cerrahoğlu in the "Intellectual Viewpoint" section of the daily *Milliyet* on June 28, 1996, Çetin Altan, a left-wing intellectual and columnist in the daily *Sabah*, was put on trial for "insulting the state" under Article 159 of the penal code for the following statement: "I want the state to cease being a gang and base itself on the rule of law."[186] The journalist who conducted the interview, Ms. Cerrahoğlu, and her responsible editor, Eren Güvener, were tried on the same charges. All were acquitted in January 1997.

• On June 26, 1996, Ali Bayramoğlu, columnist at the Istanbul daily *Yeni Yüzyıl,* and his responsible editor, İsmet Berkan, were acquitted on charges filed under Article 312 of the penal code for a column by Mr. Bayramoğlu, "Why Was Ahmet Altan Sent Away?" ("Ahmet Altan Niçin Gönderildi").[187] Mr. Bayramoğlu questioned the firing of the columnist Ahmet Altan by the daily *Milliyet* after Mr. Altan was charged under Article 312 for a column he wrote in the April 17, 1995, issue of *Milliyet*, "Father Kurd."[188] Mr. Bayramoğlu told Human Rights Watch that, "I was

---

[186]Serpil Gündüz and Miyase İlknur, "Düşünce sözde özgür" ("So-called Freedom of Expression"), *Cumhuriyet,* October 25, 1996. Altan stated that, "Ben istiyorum ki, devlet çete olmaktan çıkıp, hukuka otursun."

[187]Article 312.1 prohibits and penalizes those who "openly praise an action considered criminal" and Article 312.2 punishes those who "openly incite people to enmity and hatred by pointing to class, racial, religious, confessional, or regional difference."

[188]In the column, "Atakürt" ("Father Kurd"), Mr. Altan turned the founding myth of the Turkish republic on its head. Instead of Turks, according to Mr. Altan, Kurds founded the republic and in gratitude named their leader "Father Kurd," a play on the title granted to Mustafa Kemal, *Atatürk* ("Father Turk"). In Mr. Altan's spoof, Turks are referred to as "Sea Kurds" and forbidden to use their language. Throughout the 1980s, Kurds were often dismissed as "mountain Turks." Mr. Altan was given a one year eight month

acquitted. The prosecutor said, "Criticizing state policy is not the same as criticizing the state."[189]

- In January 1997, Mete Göktürk, a prosecutor at the Istanbul State Security Court, was arraigned under Article 159 for an October 14, 1996, article he wrote for the daily *Yeni Yüzyıl* and an appearance he made on the November 8, 1996, program of the political talk show, "Siyaset Meydanı." Mr. Göktürk complained that the Higher Council of Judges and Prosecutors (*Hâkimler ve Savcılar Yüksek Kurulu-HSYK*), which appoints judges and prosecutors and regulates their professional life, was not independent from political manipulation.[190] In a decision to send the case to the High Court of Appeals for prosecution, a lower court argued that Mr. Göktürk's statements, "did not comply with the requirements of his official title and could cause a false and denigrating understanding and interpretation of the moral personality of the Justice Ministry and the Higher Council of Judges and Prosecutors..."[191] Mr. Göktürk was eventually acquitted of these charges.

Restrictions on Reporting the Conflict in Southeastern Turkey 1987-1995

Since 1984, southeastern Turkey, largely inhabited by ethnic Kurds, has been the scene of armed conflict between government security forces and the PKK (Workers' Party of Kurdistan). A militant armed Kurdish group, the PKK has voiced explicit claims ranging from complete independence to regional autonomy within Turkey. Although no independently-confirmed figures exist, between 1984 and 1996 the government reported that 23,000 individuals had been killed in the conflict, including 13,878 PKK members, 4,310 civilians, and 2,917 government soldiers. Since early 1996, the fighting has reduced in intensity and moved to

---

suspended sentence in October 1995 along with a TL500,000 (U.S. $10) fine.

[189]Interview, Istanbul, November 1997.

[190]M. Mete Göktürk, "Yargı içinde yargısız infaz yapılıyor!" ("Extrajudicial Acts are Committed Inside the Judiciary!"), *Yeni Yüzyıl*, October 14, 1996.Mr. Göktürk also criticized the fact that *HSYK* decisions cannot be appealed

Mr.Göktürk is also a gifted political cartoonist whose drawings are collected in *Karikatür Albümü: Sen Işine Bak.*

[191]Decision number 1997/32, Beyoğlu Heavy Penalty Court No. 1, March 18, 1997.

remote mountain areas or to Northern Iraq. The PKK, while weakened, still maintains the ability to operate.

In July 1987, ten provinces in the region were placed under emergency rule because of an increase in fighting. This strict decree gave security forces special powers, including the right to hold security detainees in incommunicado detention for up to thirty days and to restrict the press. In July 1998, the parliament of Turkey approved a four-month extension of the state of emergency in the following provinces: Diyarbakır, Hakkari, Siirt, Şirnak, Tunceli and Van.

The conflict has been characterized by severe human rights abuses by both security forces and the PKK. In 1992, the government intensified a counterinsurgency campaign against the PKK, forcibly evacuating and burning rural villages. The majority of the more than 2,500 villages and hamlets depopulated in the region since 1984 are believed to be the result of this campaign. Credible estimates put the number of displaced at 560,000. The PKK in turn launched attacks against both security forces and villages that had joined the government civil-defense "village guard" program, killing village guards and their families alike. The group also assassinated those suspected of cooperating with the state, such as teachers, civil servants, and former PKK members. A wave of so-called "actor unknown murders" struck Kurdish-nationalist intellectuals and journalists as well as suspected PKK members, with the number of such deaths rising to more than 1,200 between 1992 and 1995. Credible evidence points to the fact that these "actor unknown murders" were carried out by groups operating with or under the connivance of security forces.[192]

With each new year of fighting, journalists faced increasing pressure from both the state and the PKK. A Diyarbakır-based journalist working at a mainstream daily for the past fourteen years, noted that, "There is a conflict, two sides are fighting with guns, with weapons. But there is a psychological side to the conflict. And that is important. They didn't want journalists to make objective reporting. Period. Both sides did it from time to time."[193]

Reporting conducted through 1990 could only be dreamed about in 1992. Stories filed from the region in 1992 were, for the most part, impossible to write three or four years later. The vigorous investigative journalism of the late 1980s, such as reporting by *Cumhuriyet's* Celal Başlangıç about an episode in which gendarmerie troops forced villagers to eat human excrement, is a journalistic

---

[192]See section, "VIOLENCE AGAINST JOURNALISTS: Political Killings."
[193]Interview, Diyarbakır, August 1997.

relic.[194] A Diyarbakır-based reporter for an Istanbul daily complained that, "From 1984 to 1987, it was easy to work as a journalist. You basically went where you wanted and there were no problems. After the PKK attacks increased, there were limits. After OHAL [State of Emergency Rule] was introduced in 1987, it became even harder to get information. After a while, 1990 or so, there was one source to get information, which was the emergency governor's office."[195] By the end of 1993, journalism, for the most part, was practiced in name only.

Three main reasons account for the collapse of journalism in southeastern Turkey: political violence; restrictive laws; intimidation from both the state and the PKK.

As previously discussed, political violence claimed the lives of twenty-nine journalists in Turkey between 1992-95.[196] The majority were murdered in southeastern Turkey by shadowy "counter-guerilla" and "Hizbullah" deaths squads believed by many to be linked to, or tolerated by, security forces, though the PKK is believed to have murdered five. At the height of the killings in early 1993, the weekly of the *Turkish Daily News* stated that, "It is evident, however, that without a degree of local official cooperation, carrying out attacks against this newspaper or its staff would not be possible—not, at least, without any culprits being caught." [197] Yılmaz Odabaşı, a journalist and writer, who worked in Diyarbakır during the height of the killings in 1992-93, stated that,

> I was afraid. In 1993, I left Diyarbakır because of this. Counter-guerillas were looking for me...I was in the office of the newspaper. It was in 1993, around 5-6 p.m. I had two guns with me. Two men came to my door. They said that they were from

---

[194]The villagers later appealed to the European Court of Human Rights of the Council of Europe in Strasbourg. The court found Turkey guilty of violating the European Convention on Human Rights and ordered it to pay damages to the villagers.

[195]Interview, Diyarbakır, August 1997.

[196]Most of those killed worked for radical far-left papers or for Kurdish-nationalist publications with an editorial policy sympathetic to the PKK, such as *Özgür Gündem* or one of its predecessors or successor publications. For a more in-depth discussion, see section, "VIOLENCE AGAINST JOURNALISTS: Political Killings."

[197]"Özgür Gündem Bids Farewell,"*Turkish Probe*, Ankara, January 19, 1993. For a period of about three years, from 1991-1994, the English-language daily *Turkish Daily News* provided the best day-to-day coverage on the conflict in southeastern Turkey. İsmet İmset, forced into political exile in London after running afoul of authorities, provided much of this reporting.

the Security Directorate. I call the Security Directorate, they said that they didn't send anybody. I didn't open the door obviously. That is what prompted me to leave Diyarbakır.[198]

The second impediment was legal. A number of long-standing prohibitions threatened journalists with imprisonment for writing critical stories.[199] Furthermore, most of the provinces that comprise the ethnically Kurdish areas of southeastern Turkey had been placed under emergency rule since 1987.[200] The situation worsened in April 1990, when the Council of Ministers under then Prime Minister Turgut Özal passed Decree 413, the so-called "Censor and Exile Decree" (*Sansür ve Sürgün Kararnamesi*).[201] Among other powers, Decree 413 and subsequent decrees that replaced it gave the Emergency Rule Governor the power to ban and confiscate publications and close the printing houses. The decree threatened penalties against publications that, "wrongly represent incidents occurring in a region under a state of emergency, disturb[ing] its readers with distorted news stories or commentaries, caus[ing] anxiety among people in the region and obstruct[ing] security forces in the performance of their jobs."[202] The decree had the effect of prior censorship: editors refused to run stories that they feared would lead to a closure of the paper and printing house.[203] Although in December 1990 and May 1991 the Constitutional Court ruled that Decree 413 and

---

[198]Interview, Ankara, August 1997. Journalists have the right to carry a gun in Turkey. Mr. Odabaşı relates his experiences in the book, *To be a Journalist in the Southeast* (*Güneydoğu'da Gazeteci Olmak*), published in 1994.

[199]*See* "Domestic Law."

[200]Emergency rule was declared on July 14, 1987, when decree (KHK) No. 285 was published in the *Official Gazette*. At present, Diyarbakır, Hakkari, Siirt, Şirnak, Tunceli, and Van provinces are under a state of emergency.

[201]Such decrees have the force of law (*KHK-Kanun hükmünde kararname*). They become law when approved by parliament and published in the *Official Gazette*.

[202]For information on Decree 413, see Helsinki Watch, "News from Turkey," June 1990, p. 2. Decree 413 was later superseded by Decrees 424, 425, and finally by Decree 430, which softened some of the harsher aspects of the earlier decrees, such as abolishing the penalty of indefinite closure of a printing house that violates the decree. See *Kürt Çıkmazı*, p. 57 and Department of State, *Country Report on Human Rights Practices for 1990*, (Washington, D.C.: United States Government Printing Office, 1991), p. 1294.

[203]In his book, *Kürt Çıkmazı (Kurdish Dead-end)*, Koray Düzgören publishes several stories that he wrote at the time but which could not be published in the now defunct daily *Güneş* because of Decree 413.

its successors were unconstitutional, the decisions were not published in the *Official Gazette*—thus giving them the force of law—until 1992.[204]

Finally, neither security authorities in the region nor the PKK trust journalists, and both sides try to use the press to its own ends. Police are extremely suspicious of reporters, whom they view as needless meddlers and troublemakers.[205] One Diyarbakır-based journalist working for an Istanbul daily complained that, "No threats of late, but sometimes the security forces deal with us in a tough manner. Sometimes they hit you, give you dirty looks. About twenty days ago, at the airport, a policeman told me, 'If this wasn't a public place I would show you.'"[206] Another griped that, "I have been threatened by the police, film confiscated, beaten. The past couple of years, no beating. But this year, last year, they took our film. The reason was that we had met with the PKK. But the real reason was that they wanted to get pictures of the PKK."[207] The editor of the Turkish-Kurdish bilingual weekly *Hêvi*, stated that,

> We have an office in Diyarbakır, but outside of Diyarbakır we do not have an office because of pressure from the authorities. We have reporters, but they can't show their press cards that we issue them. That will bring even more harassment from the police. When they see it they say we are terrorists.[208]

When detained, journalists are often mistreated by the police.

The PKK has mirrored the repressive attitude toward journalists displayed by state authorities. According to the French group Reporters sans Frontieres, "The PKK has always had a hostile attitude toward the mainstream press and private television stations because of the belief that they spy for military or intelligence

---

[204]*Türkiye İnsan Hakları Raporu 1991* (Ankara: Human Rights Foundation of Turkey, January 1992), p. 16.

[205]For an explanation of police-press relations and police violence against the press, *see* "Violence against Journalists: Beatings."

[206]Interview, Diyarbakır, August 1997.

[207]Interview, Diyarbakır, August 1997.

[208]Interview with Fehmi Işık, editor of *Hêvi*, Istanbul, August 1997. For more on *Hêvi*, *see*, "Restrictions on the Use of the Kurdish Language."

organizations."[209] In October 1993, the PKK ordered all the Diyarbakır-based bureau chiefs of the mainstream dailies to gather at a camp outside of Diyarbakır and ordered them to cease operations because of their "biased and one-sided reporting... which favored state forces and acted like the henchmen of the...Emergency Rule Governor."[210] If their offices remained open, the PKK warned that the journalists would became "revolutionary targets."[211] With few exceptions, almost all the papers closed their bureaus until mid-1994.[212]

The PKK has also threatened journalists who wrote unfavorably about their struggle. One journalist based in Diyarbakır for an Istanbul daily reported that,

> There are threats from both sides. When you go to the PKK side and try to interview them, they say, "You are not writing the truth." I wrote one story. The PKK didn't like it so they threatened me. In the end, nothing happened. Even though we are Kurds, we work at mainstream papers and they do not trust us.[213]

Another ethnic-Kurdish journalist who reported from the southeast stated that,

> I wrote an article once criticizing Öcalan for his inflated statements and the cult of personality around him. After this article was published, two or three young guys came to me. They pushed me against the wall and said, "If you are not careful with

---

[209] *Türkiye Kayıp Düşler.*

In May 1998, after an assassination attempt against Akin Birdal, the head of the Human Rights Association of Turkey, the ERNK, the political wing of the PKK, made the following threat against arch-conservative *Hürriyet* columnist Emin Çölaşan, Kemalist İlhan Selçuk of the daily *Cumhuriyet,* and the chairman of the Press Council of Turkey, Oktay Ekşi: "In the future, we will not be so hesitant in using our right of defense." "PKK'dan Çirkin Tehdit," *Hürriyet* (Internet Edition), May 14, 1998.

[210] "Consolidating Its Hold: PKK Bans Press in Southeast," *Turkish Probe*, Ankara, October 26, 1993, p. 6.

[211] Ibid.

[212] The PKK ban did not include the Kurdish-nationalist *Özgür Gündem.* That publication, however, had its own problems in the form of police harassment and shadowy death squads.

The ban was reportedly lifted a month or so after its imposition. By mid-1994, most of the closed news bureaus had reopened.

[213] Interview, Diyarbakır, August 1997.

your pen we will destroy you." They were PKK, no doubt, but I don't know for sure if the PKK officially sent them. Once before I was threatened by the PKK. I wrote an article which was critical of certain aspects of their violence. Shortly thereafter I received a call from a PKK member who told me, "If you continue to do 'reformism' you should leave Diyarbakır." It's funny, because when the PKK was threatening me, the death squads were threatening me, too.[214]

The PKK also has conducted a policy of kidnapping journalists who do not acquire "press credentials" from the ERNK, the political wing of the PKK. Since 1994, five journalists have been kidnapped; two were held for three months.[215] The kidnapping of journalists, like that of foreign tourists, serves as a propaganda stunt to show that the ARGK, the military wing of the PKK, can operate in the southeast. As one local journalist explained:

Some journalists have been kidnapped and taken to the mountains at a PKK roadblock. Journalists have to get permission from the ERNK. They kidnap the journalist to make propaganda, say that we control the region, then they try to protect them from getting killed until the journalist is released.[216]

The ARGK's ability to kidnap journalist has been reduced along with their diminished military capacity in the region. The last kidnapping occurred on April 30, 1995, when Ferit Demir, a freelance journalist in Tunceli province, was held by the PKK for a little over a week . The previous kidnapping took place in March 1995, when an ARGK unit held AFP journalist Kadri Gürsel and Reuters photographer Fati Sarıbaş for twenty-six days.[217]

---

[214]Interview, Bursa, November 1997.

[215]*Türkiye Kayıp Düşler*. Kutlu Esendemir and Levent Öztürk, both working for TGRT state television, were kidnapped on January 26, 1994, and not released until April 26, 1994.

[216]Interview, Diyarbakır, August 1997.

[217]Mr. Gürsel wrote an excellent book about his experience that provides valuable insights into the motivations and tactics of PKK fighters and units. See, *Dağdakiler* (*Those in the Mountains*), (Istanbul: Siyahbeyaz Series, Metis Publishing, June 1996).

The Present Situation

Present reporting on the fourteen-year conflict in southeastern Turkey is sketchy, at best. Despite the fact that almost all the major Turkish dailies have offices in Diyarbakır, most daily reporting now consists of republishing statements on PKK casualties issued by the Office of the Emergency Rule Governor.[218] When more detailed stories are written, they often deal with non-controversial topics, such as an article about the grand opening of a tennis court in Tunceli province, a scene of heavy fighting and wide scale displacement.[219] Stories that attempt to deal with more sensitive topics often skirt delicate issues: an article on the displaced states that they left their homes "because of terror" without any further examination of that issue.[220]

The military has also begun to organize press tours, but this effort is aimed more at public relations than at facilitating good journalism. Oktay Ekşi, head of the Press Council of Turkey and chief columnist at *Hürriyet*, summed up the present situation as follows: "You learn something by chance in the southeast. You learn only what the government allows you to learn. That region is in darkness. Unfortunately, you can't see the real facts in the southeast....The cost is very high."[221]

---

[218]For example, "37 PKK'li öldürüldü" ("37 PKK Members Killed"), *Milliyet* (Internet Edition), June 9, 1998. The story states that, "In a statement made yesterday by the State of Emergency Region Governor's Office, 23 terrorists were killed in the Kelmehmet mountain region of Şırnak...for a total of 37 terrorists killed." It gives no analysis of the information or additional sources to confirm official statements. Consequently casualty figures reported by the military—along with those announced by the PKK—enjoy little credibility.

[219]See "Tunceli'de tenis," ("Tennis in Tunceli"), *Hürriyet*, August 28, 1997. A mountainous region bordering northeast and southeast Anatolia, Tunceli has witnessed heavy fighting since 1993 and suffered wide-scale displacement, most the result of the military's counterinsurgency campaign. According to the 1990 census, Tunceli province had a population of 133,143. In 1997, its population had shrunk to 82,535. While the province has been losing population for years because of economic migration, the majority of the population decline in the 1990-97 period is due to the conflict.

[220]A. Ressak Oral, "Şimdi de geriye dönüş sıkıntısı" ("Even Now There is a Problem with the Return"), *Milliyet,* July 28, 1995.

A good example of such journalism is the "Let's Go Southeast" press campaign initiated by the mainstream daily *Milliyet* in the summer of 1998. The reporting deals with issues that are considered safe, such as unemployment and under-development. It does little, however, to explore the ethnic or political aspects of the conflict.

[221]Interview, Istanbul, August 1997.

From time to time, however, journalists do manage to travel to the region to conduct independent reporting, and columnists sometimes write unvarnished accounts of the strife, based on first-hand information.[222] Two stories by *Cumhuriyet* correspondent Celal Yılmaz on alleged abuses by Special Team members in the Varto district of Bingöl province provide an example of good reporting under tough circumstances. His reporting is based on multiple sources and on eyewitness testimony and seeks to verify independently statements given by state officials. In one of his columns in *Cumhuriyet*, Hikmet Çetinkaya quotes at length the parents of a young man, Mazlum Mansuroğlu, who was allegedly detained and murdered by security forces in Tunceli province. In addition, parliamentarians will sometimes travel to the region to investigate the situation, and the journalists who accompany them will report their often critical findings unfiltered. Such reporting is certainly the exception, not the rule.

Lack of access to the region—especially to scenes of fighting in rural areas—was the major complaint of Diyarbakır-based journalists. Over time, the area in which journalists can move freely has been reduced to Diyarbakır and certain provincial capitals in the region. Rural areas have largely become a no-go zone. No journalist, foreign or Turkish, has been able to enter Northern Iraq since 1996 save for an occasional press pool organized and guided by the Turkish Army. In February 1997, the *New York Times* Istanbul bureau chief was detained by security forces for a day near a village in Batman province and interrogated.[223] A journalist working in the Diyarbakır office of a Istanbul daily noted that,

> The regional governor sends us a fax, we accept it and write the news to the newspaper. For example, there is a fax that says that on Cudi mountain 150 PKK were killed. We don't have the possibility to go there and investigate. To see bodies, to find out details about the clash, where it happened, where are the bodies. Local people don't believe it, but the Turkish people out of the region do. If we don't write the story based on these faxes, then

---

[222]See, Celal Yılmaz, "Halk Özel Timi Suçluyor" ("The People Blame the Special Teams"), *Cumhuriyet Hafta*, November 11, 1996, and "Vartolu ilçeyi terk ediyor" ("The People of Varto are Abandoning Their District"), *Cumhuriyet Hafta*, December 5, 1996.

See Hikmet Çetinkaya, "Mazlum!...," *Cumhuriyet Hafta*, August 23, 1996. In a black twist, "Mazlum," the murdered man's name, means "oppressed."

[223]Interview with Stephen Kinzer, Istanbul, August 1997; "American Reporter Detained by Turks," Associated Press, March 1997. Mr. Kinzer had participated in a military-organized press tour and then stayed on in the region after the official tour ended.

the Anatolian News Agency sends out the story and our editors complain to us why we didn't write the story.[224]

Another journalist working in Diyarbakır for a mainstream daily had similar problems:

> Sometimes you could follow the village evacuations. You went to a village. [Now] it is impossible to go to the scene of an armed clash or the scene of an incident....[you can go] only if the regional governor gives you his permission. You end up with an organized trip....So, for example, if I wanted to go to Lice, I would get sent back at the first checkpoint. I tried to go to Tunceli yesterday. I was "given" a policeman and he followed me the entire time. It is difficult to be a journalist on your own. At the border to Tunceli province, they [the authorities] take your press card and give you a policeman.[225]

The Confiscation of Publications and Books and the Closing of Newspapers [226]

Both the constitution and the Press Law give prosecutors the power to stop distribution of a publication without previously obtaining a court order.[227] A judge,

---

[224]Interview, Diyarbakır, August 1997. Anatolian News Agency is the semi-official wire service.

[225]Interview, Diyarbakır, August 1997.

[226]In Turkish law, a distinction is made between "periodicals" (*mevkute* or *süreli*) and all other types of publication (*süresiz* or *mevkute tanımına girmeyen basılmış eserler*). The law makes this distinction to enable prosecutors to determine criminal responsibility where there is no responsible editor. *See also* Article 16 of the Press Law in the Appendix.

By law, a printer must bring all published material after its release to the Collection Office of the Security Directorate *(Derleme Bürosu)*. The publication is registered, quickly scanned, and sent on to the state prosecutor if it is believed to have violated the law. Stephen Kinzer, the *New York Times* Istanbul bureau chief, interviewed a state official who culls the press for offending articles. See "A Terror to Journalists, He Sniffs Out Terrorists," *New York Times*, September 1, 1997.

[227]Article 28.5 of the constitution states that,

> ....By taking the proper measures, distribution is stopped by a judge's decision; in situations where problems could arise because of a delay, [distribution] can also be prevented by the order of an authority so empowered by the law. The proper authority that prevented publication must inform the relevant judge within twenty-

however, must ratify the prosecutor's action within forty-eight hours or it becomes invalid. A judge may also confiscate a publication for reasons of national security or if a criminal investigation has been opened against it.[228] Acts triggering confiscation are broadly defined as threats to "the internal or external security of the state... which tend to incite offense, riot or insurrection." Under the 1961 constitution, in contrast, prosecutors did not have the power to confiscate publications. Law No. 1488, passed five months after the March 1971 coup, however, amended the constitution to give prosecutors that power. This change was carried over into the 1982 constitution.

Periodicals may be temporarily closed by a court order if the writers at the publication have been convicted of certain crimes, such as threatening the unity of

---

four hours. If the relevant judge does not confirm this order at the latest within forty-eight hours, the decision preventing publication is invalid....

Additional Article 1 of the Press Law states that,

The distribution of any type of periodical or non-periodical publication that contains crimes outlined in the Second Book, first chapter, 1st, 2nd, and fourth paragraphs or in Articles 311 or 312 or secret information belonging to the state can be prevented by the decision of a local justice of the peace judge *(sulh ceza)* or, in cases where delay would cause a problem, by the written decision of a local republican prosecutor's office. The republican prosecutor's office must inform the police court magistrate of its decision at the latest within twenty-four hours. At the latest within forty-eight hours the police court magistrate will give a decision either confirming or overturning this decision. In case of non-approval, the decision of the state prosecutor's office is invalid....

[228]Article 28.7 of the constitution states that,

Periodicals and non-periodical publications can be confiscated by a judge's decision in those circumstances when the crimes investigation has started and by the order of an authority so empowered by the law in cases of protecting the state's indivisible unity with the country and nation, national security, public order, general morality, and with the goal of preventing a crime where problems could arise because of a delay. The proper authority that gave the confiscation order must inform the relevant judge within twenty-four hours. If the relevant judge does not confirm this order at the latest within forty-eight hours, the decision preventing publication is invalid...

the state.[229] In addition, publications that are deemed a continuation of banned publications are forbidden. Additional Article 2.2 of the 1950 Press Law (No. 7564) sets the temporary period of closure from three days to one month.[230] In 1983, shortly before the military relinquished power to a civilian government, the press law was amended to include Article 2.2.[231]

Prosecutors primarily, though not exclusively, target far-left and Kurdish-nationalist publications—especially those whose editorial policy sympathizes with armed groups, such as the PKK or the armed extremist-left group Dev-Sol. In 1996, the French media watch-dog group Reporters Sans Frontieres (RSF) reported that on twenty-nine different occasions twenty newspapers or other periodicals were suspended from publishing for varying periods of time.[232] In addition, fifty-three daily, weekly, or monthly periodicals faced confiscation 201 times in 1996.[233] In 1997, RSF reported the following figures: on thirty-four different occasions thirty-one publications were suspended from publishing for varying periods of

---

[229]Article 28.10 of the constitution states that,

> By court order, periodicals that are published in Turkey and are sentenced in cases dealing with the state's indivisible unity with its country and state, the basic principles of the republic, national security, or violation of general morality can be temporarily closed. Every publication that is openly the continuation of a closed periodical is forbidden; such periodicals can be confiscated by a judge's decision.

[230]Additional Article 2 states that,

> A periodical publication can be closed by a court for a period of three days to one month if that publication is sentenced for crimes outlined in additional Article 1, or for behavior contradictory to national security or general morality. Every type of publication that is openly a continuation of a closed periodical is forbidden. One who continues to publish a closed publication or who publishes a new periodical that is clearly the continuation of a closed publication according to the first paragraph will be punished with imprisonment of one to six months and a heavy fine of from 100,000 to 300,000 lira.

[231] Under provisional Article 15 of the constitution, legislation cannot be found unconstitutional that was passed between the coup of September 12, 1980, and the convening of parliament after the first post-coup elections which were held in 1983. Such legislation can only be changed if the government passes a law to replace or amend it.

[232] RSF, *Rapport Annuel 1997*, Internet Edition.

[233]Ibid.

time; thirty-three daily, weekly, or monthly periodicals faced confiscation seventy-eight times.[234]

Confiscation and closure cases include the following:

•   On August 16, 1995, the fifth Istanbul Penal Court closed down the Kurdish-nationalist daily *Yeni Politika* under Article 2.2 of the press law because it was deemed to be a continuation of its banned predecessor, *Özgür Ülke*. That newspaper had been closed under the same law in February 1995.

•   On May 9, 1996, the now defunct, left-wing daily *Evrensel* was suspended from publishing for seventy-five days by order of the Istanbul State Security Court; the paper was deemed to have violated Article 312 of the penal code, which prohibits incitement of hatred based on ethnicity, religion, race, or confession, because of an interview with an army officer who alleged that he had carried out reprisals in southeastern Turkey

•   On February 17, 1997, the mainstream-liberal daily *Radikal* was confiscated by order of a prosecutor. Its offense was to republish an Islamist critique of the role of Atatürk that appeared on February 15 in the mainstream French publication, *Le Figaro Magazine*. The article was deemed to violate a 1951 law protecting the legacy of Atatürk.

•   On September 8, 1997, Istanbul State Security Court No. 2 banned the publication of Celal Alî Bedirxan's 1934 work *On the Kurdish Question (Kürt Sorunu Üzerine)* by a small, independent Kurdish publisher, Avesta.[235]

•   On May 8, 1998, the High Court of Appeals confirmed a ten-day closure of the Kurdish- nationalist daily, *Ülkede Gündem*. The paper was closed because of an August 4, 1997, article by the chairman of the now-banned

---

[234] RSF, *Rapport Annuel 1998*, Internet Edition.
[235] Istanbul State Security Court No. 2, Confiscation Order, 1997/310, September 8, 1997.

Kurdish nationalist Democracy Party titled, "The Tragedy of Dersim." The court ruled that the article violated Article 312 of the penal code.[236]

Even overtly non-political works can, at times, run afoul of the authorities. Emre Yılmaz's wry, inside look at Istanbul high-finance and big business, *A Young Businessman (Genç bir İşadamı)*, was temporarily banned in 1996 on morals charges. [237]

Self-censorship[238]

Self-censorship is a fact of life in Turkey, whether one speaks of the mainstream press or of Kurdish-nationalist publications sympathetic to the PKK. In the case of the mainstream press, self-censorship is motivated by two main factors: fear of prosecution and an internalized deference to state authority on the part of the editors. In the case of the Kurdish-nationalist press, self-censorship manifests itself as fealty—either imposed or voluntary—to a purported higher political cause.

In the Mainstream Press

Self-censorship is imposed when writing on a number of sensitive topics, such as the proper role of the military, political Islam, the conflict in southeastern Turkey, the Kurdish minority, and the events surrounding the 1915 expulsion from eastern Turkey and subsequent massacre of large numbers of ethnic Armenians by the Ottoman government.[239] Self-censorship is largely a function of the overall

---

[236]"Ülkede Gündem Newspaper Closed for Ten Days," *Turkish Daily News*, Internet Edition, May 12, 1998; Human Rights Foundation of Turkey, Daily Bulletin, May 11, 1998.

[237]The book was confiscated on June 4, 1996, allegedly because it violated Article 426 of the penal code. That provision punishes one who, in the press or in theater or film, "offends the public's sense of shame and modesty or incites and exploits sexual desires... ." One offending statement from the book contained the phrase, "I'm forty and my you-know-what still can get as hard as a rock upon waking." Upon appeal, a court overturned the confiscation order three weeks later. See a short pamphlet Mr. Yılmaz published, *Hukuk Sergüzeşti (A Legal Adventure)*, which contains the confiscation order, his defense, expert witness testimony, and the court order overturning the confiscation.

[238]*See also*, "The Role of the Media"

[239]The Republic of Armenia, diaspora Armenians, and some Westerners refer to these events as a "genocide." Most Western scholars of the Ottoman Empire acknowledge the expulsion of Armenian communities from eastern Anatolia and the subsequent massacre of many of those uprooted, but point to the fact that it is unclear in the absence of archival

climate: there is less during more liberal periods and more when outside restrictions are tightened. Some top-level columnists told Human Rights Watch that they never resorted to self-censorship, while others said they did. Self-censorship operates on at least two different levels: by journalists and by columnists when they write the actual piece; and, later, by editors.

Many journalists reported that—at the very least—they were cognizant of the boundaries and of how far these boundaries might be pushed without evoking a legal response. Ahmet Altan, a popular novelist and columnist for the daily *Yeni Yüzyıl,* stated that, "Among the administration of the press, there is self-censorship. Among the writers, it depends." Younger, lesser known journalists appear acutely aware of limitations and the need to pay fealty to them. A Diyarbakır-based correspondent for a mainstream daily complained that, "Some practice self-censorship, others do not. I try not to. If something happens, I write a story. But I don't write a story if I am sure that it will not be published."[240] An Istanbul-based journalist working at a mainstream daily reported that, "There are a lot of young journalists who want to reveal facts, but the editors tell them, 'Don't bring me news like this.'"[241]

Some older, more popular columnists, on the other hand, are less easily intimidated. Oktay Ekşi, the chief columnist for the mainstream daily *Hürriyet,* stated that, "I personally have the right to write what I want."

Other high-ranking, popular columnists disagree, while admitting that they have a large degree of latitude. Oral Çalışlar, a columnist at the Istanbul daily *Cumhuriyet,* complained that,

> We journalists think about whether we will get into trouble if we criticize things like drug dealing connected with the war. Especially if it is aimed at a high level....I write everyday, and I am being careful not to commit a crime. If I were to write completely freely, I could have a court case against me....But I am one of the people who has the fewest limits. Even though I am not afraid of violating them, it is a factor.[242]

---

proof whether the act was "genocide." For its part, the government of Turkey and some scholars argue that communal violence took the lives of Muslims and Armenians alike.

Until the government of Turkey allows full and unhindered access to Ottoman archives, no definitive answer can be reached, including on the number of those killed.

[240]Interview, Diyarbakır, September 1997.

[241]Interview, Istanbul, September 1997.

[242]Interview, Istanbul, August 1997.

Koray Düzgören, a former columnist at the daily *Radikal* and long-time journalist, noted that, "Even me personally, I question myself. If I timidly support what I believe in [because of the need for self-censorship], I pull my article.[243]

A second level of self-censorship is imposed by editors, who act as a filter to screen out stories that may cause problems. Often they serve as conduits for the interests of newspaper owners.[244] Mr. Düzgören commented that: "The main pressure....is from ourselves and our editors. In many cases, if people took a stand, the state would not care."[245] A young journalist who worked at the daily *Yeni Yüzyıl* described the dilemma in which editors found themselves when they wanted to adopt a more critical tone:

> For example, I worked at *Yeni Yüzyıl* for about a year, directly after it started publication. It started as a good paper and really took on sensitive issues, like the Kurdish question. But soon the editors working there began to have conflicted feelings. They wanted to be more sensitive, but they started not to want to write such critical things. To write news about torture means that you criticize the state, which means that you are a leftist. The stories the editor-in-chief rejected would be given to the news editor, who would try to publish it. He would publish it, but then he got in trouble and the practice stopped.[246]

Often the pressure comes from editors indirectly, in the form of suggestions or hints. A well-known columnist at an Istanbul daily reported velvet-gloved pressure from his editor in an effort to force him to stop writing about the now-banned Islamist Welfare (*Refah*) Party:

> Up to six months ago [April 1997] I could do all I wanted, then I had to start to limit myself. That didn't happen with direct warnings, but I am in close contact with my executives. Not a censorship mechanism but an "autocensorship" mechanism. For example, when Refah was in power my editors wanted me to

---

[243]Interview, Istanbul, August 1997.
[244]*See also*, "The Role of the Media."
[245]Interview, Istanbul, August 1997.
[246]Interview, Istanbul, September 1997.

stop writing about them. I was trying to write about them objectively.[247]

In the Kurdish-Nationalist Press

Self-censorship also affects "pro-Kurdish" or "Kurdish-nationalist" newspapers and publications. As one ethnic Kurdish observer commented, "The status of the Kurdish establishment and the Turkish establishment are largely the same: self-limiting and censoring. Whatever is going on in the Turkish circles is going on in the Kurdish circles."[248] Usually, the self-censorship comes in the form of suppressing news or information that is critical of a Kurdish political faction, usually the PKK. A young, liberal journalist working at a mainstream paper commented that,

> There is no difference between *Sabah, Hürriyet,* and *Gündem* in the following respect. Each paper has the right to make news according to its political beliefs and editorial policy. The news that they report and the way that they report it are different. In the first days of *Özgür Gündem* they wrote, "Our side captured a Jandarma station." We know where they are coming from. They are supporting an organization through their thoughts. It is their legal right. *Hürriyet* does the same, but they do not pay a price [to the state]. As a result of not paying the price of self-censorship to one side, they pay the price of self-censorship to the other side. Mainstream papers have self-censorship.[249]

---

[247]Interview, Istanbul, November 1997. The columnist asked not to be identified. A coalition-government led by the Welfare Party was forced to resign under intense military pressure on June 18, 1997. In early 1998, the party was banned and its leader, Mr. Necmettin Erbakan, along with several other leaders, were banned from politics for five years. *See also,* "The Role of the Military."

[248]Interview, September 1997 in Turkey. The individual asked not to be identified.

[249]Interview, Istanbul, September 1997.

Sabah and *Hürriyet* are mainstream papers whose coverage is often crudely nationalistic and blindly pro-state regarding the conflict in southeastern Turkey. In both papers, however, individual columnists and journalists can and do take a critical, hard-hitting line on sensitive issues. *Ülkede Gündem,* now banned, adopted an editorial line that initially was critical in general and later became sympathetic to the goals if not the methods of the PKK.

Two journalists working at *Ülkede Gündem,* a daily pro-Kurdish newspaper published in Istanbul, differed on whether self-censorship existed: one admitted to Human Rights Watch that it did exist, while the other denied such allegations outright.[250]

The PKK's intolerant attitude toward dissident voices has fostered self-censorship among Kurdish intellectuals and Kurdish publications. One observer of the Kurdish question in Turkey complained that, "Last year I went to Germany for a conference of Kurdish intellectuals. They face a major problem: speaking about their own matters and problems without having to mention the PKK. In private they are open and critical, but in public different. The situation is worse in journals that are sympathetic to the PKK."[251]

A Kurdish intellectual who has been jailed by the state for writing about the conflict in the southeast and about Turkey's Kurds, lamented that,

> In order to end the official ideology, they [the PKK] have become an official ideology that is closed to debate. In what I write I criticize their making arbitrary attacks, placing bombs in buses, taking hostages, killing village guard (*korucu*) families and children. In fighting between the donkey and the horse, the chickens get trampled....I really felt this pain as a Kurdish intellectual who lived there for many years. It is sad that the PKK has absolutely no tolerance for a critical approach. The Kurds cannot be a unitary entity because the PKK is against so many Kurdish intellectuals. The PKK calls Kemal Burkay a traitor. They call the party of Serafettin Elçi a "korucu" party. The PKK has left no choice to Kurdish intellectuals but to applaud them. It reminds me of a line by Baudelier: "The wound is ours, the knife is ours, the victim is ours, the assassin is ours." We grew up in a semi-feudal environment. The state has despotic tendencies. I don't want Aşiret [tribal] authority, I don't want PKK authority, I don't want state authority.[252]

Ahmet Altan, the writer and columnist, summed up the dilemma of Kurdish intellectuals:

---

[250]Interview, Istanbul, August 1997.
[251]Interview with Koray Düzgören, Istanbul, August 1997.
[252]Interview, Ankara, August 1997.

There is self-censorship in the Kurdish press. This happens both to Kurdish intellectuals and Turkish intellectuals. We should see that they face difficulties themselves. I do not do that, I write the way I like. But, both Kurdish and Turkish intellectuals limit themselves, censor themselves. But the situation is different. They fire me, they sue me. When they fire me, I become some sort of a hero among those who choose to limit themselves. I am not left alone, I receive respect. When I dare to dispute my political authority, I become a "hero." When a Kurdish intellectual challenges his political authority he becomes a "traitor." You become a traitor against the Turkish state and also against the PKK. The Turkish intellectuals are also afraid of being declared a traitor by people of their side. But when we criticize our political authority we become respected by our friends. When they criticize their political authority they commit treason. At this point, it is impossible to understand the Turkish state. The Turkish chief of staff and PKK reinforce each other.[253]

---

[253]Interview, Istanbul, August 1997.

IX. RESTRICTIONS ON THE USE OF THE KURDISH LANGUAGE

International Legal Protections

International law protects the rights of persons to assert their membership in an ethnic minority and to express themselves in the minority's traditional language. The U.N. Declaration on the Rights of Persons Belonging to National or Ethnic, Religious and Linguistic Minorities, in particular, requires states to ensure that members of minorities "have adequate opportunities to learn their mother tongue," explaining that such persons have "the right . . . to use their own language, in private and in public, freely without interference or any form of discrimination."[254] Although the declaration lacks the binding legal force of a treaty, it constitutes an authoritative explication of existing treaty norms protecting the rights to free expression and non-discrimination.

A similar concern for protecting minority-language speakers from discrimination on the basis of language is found in the European Convention for the Protection of Human Rights and Fundamental Freedoms, which bars such discrimination with regard to all of the rights within its purvey, including the right to free expression.[255] Although the European Court on several occasions rejected the claim that language rights include the right to use the language of one's choice in communicating with public authorities, it has struck down burdens based solely on "considerations relating to language" in a decision involving French-speaking residents of the Flemish community who wanted their children to attend French-language schools.[256] In other words, the court has been reluctant to impose positive obligations on states to accommodate the linguistic preferences of their citizens, but has at the same time recognized the state obligation not to interfere in citizens' use of their language.[257] Consequently, legal obstacles in Turkey that prevent

---

[254]G.A. Res. 47/135, U.N. GAOR, 47th Sess., 3d Comm., Annex, U.N. Doc. a/47/678/Add.2 (1992).

[255](European) Convention for the Protection of Human Rights and Fundamental Freedoms, art. 14. This provision echoes Article 2 of the Universal Declaration of Human Rights, which enumerates "language" as an impermissible ground for discrimination.

[256]"Belgium Linguistic" Cases, 11 Y.B. Eur. Conv. on Human Rights 832 (1968), p. 942.

[257]For related decisions of the U.N. Human Rights Committee, see, for example, *Ballantyne, Davidson and McIntyre v. Canada*, Comm. Nos. 359/1989 and 385/1989, U.N. Doc. CCPR/C/47/D/359/1989 (1993) (finding that Quebec's restrictions on languages permitted in outdoor advertising violate international protections on freedom of expression).

individuals from administering private language courses in Kurdish or a private Kurdish-language television station would violate the intent of such rulings.

The U.N. Sub-Commission on Prevention of Discrimination and Protection of Minorities, whose mandate specifically includes the protection of linguistic minorities, has been even more active in support of language rights. In a landmark 1979 study, the sub-commission praised the efforts of numerous states that had taken steps to facilitate the use of minority languages in a variety of contexts, including in communications with state authorities.[258] It has also shown that it regards the repression of linguistic minorities to be a serious breach of international law, passing a 1993 resolution condemning Yugoslavia for banning in Kosovo "the use of the Albanian language, notably within the public administration and services."[259]

International legal protections on language, as well as the concern shown by numerous international bodies on the topic, reflect the central place of language in ethnic and cultural identity. Language is commonly taken as a prime indicator of the individual's group identification; for this reason, language repression has almost always played a role in policies of group domination and forced assimilation.

Prohibitions Against the Use of Kurdish and Languages Other than Turkish

At present, the use of languages other than Turkish in education, politics and the broadcast media is—with certain exceptions—prohibited.[260] Article 3 of the constitution declares Turkish to be the official language, while Article 42.9 goes further by stating that, "Aside from Turkish, no other language shall be studied by or taught to Turkish citizens as a mother tongue in any language, teaching, or learning institution."[261] While these strictures are, in theory, directed against all of the languages spoken by the different ethnic groups that live in Turkey, whether Circassians or Laz, the main targets are Kurds and Kurdish.

---

[258]See Sub-Commission on Prevention of Discrimination and Protection of Minorities, Study on the Rights of Persons Belonging to Ethnic, Religious and Linguistic Minorities, U.N. Doc. E/CN.4/Sub.2/384/Rev.1 (1979).

[259]U.N. Doc. E/CN.4/1993/45 (1993), para.1993/9.

[260] Since the abolition of Law No. 2932 in April 1991, no law prohibits publishing books or newspapers in Kurdish or other non-Turkish languages.

[261]Unofficial translation.

No official data exist concerning the size of ethnic minorities in Turkey since the early 1960s.[262] Despite the absence of exact data, however, it is clear that Kurds are the second largest ethnic group in Turkey after Turks, and Kurdish is the second most widely spoken language after Turkish. The absence of such data on ethnicity stems from the fact that the state has not asked questions regarding ethnicity or religion during census polling.[263] In addition, ethnicity is a rather fluid concept in Turkey.[264]

State-dictated rigidity concerning language and identity is the result of an attempt to build a modern nation-state based on a secular Turkish national identity and the Turkish language.[265] That process began in 1923, when Mustafa Kemal,

---

[262]A Turkish saying states that, "In Turkey there are seventy-two and a half people" ("Türkiye'de yetmiş iki buçuk millet var"). The phrase captures the ethnic mosaic of Turkey's population, which, aside from Turks, ranges from Kurds and Arabs living in Anatolia for hundreds of years to Chechens and Circassians who fled Tsarist persecution in the nineteenth century.

[263]Estimates regarding the size of Turkey's ethnic Kurdish population range from 10 to 20 percent of the populace. The last attempt to ascertain information concerning ethnicity and religion occurred in the early 1960s. The Ministry of Works and Settlement (İmar ve İskân Bakanlığı) and the Village Affairs Ministry (Köy İşleri Bakanlığı) conducted a nationwide survey of villages, *The Village Inventory* (*Köy Envanteri*), in which questions concerning language and religion were posed. After data for one province was released, however, the study was repressed. See Peter Alfred Andrews, ed., *Ethnic Groups in the Republic of Turkey* (Wiesbaden: Dr. Ludwig Reichert Verlag, 1989), pp. 18, 42-44.

[264]The fact that Turkey's ethnic Kurdish population is far from monolithic further complicates counting them. Martin Van Bruinessen, a leading scholar of the Kurds, notes that, "There is, then, no unambiguous ethnic boundary separating Kurds from non-Kurds, and in the course of even recent history the boundaries as perceived by various groups have shifted. Large numbers of people have moreover purposively crossed what they perceived as the major ethnic boundary, not only individually, as is wont to happen virtually everywhere, but in many cases collectively." See Martin Van Bruinessen, "The Ethnic Identity of the Kurds," p. 616, in Andrews.

[265]Linguistic and ethnic plurality had been the rule, however, in the Ottoman Empire. One scholar has noted that, "No attempt had been made to force Ottoman subjects to speak Turkish--in 1800 a large majority did not speak it as their first language and perhaps most Ottoman subjects did not speak it at all. Serbs spoke Serbian, Greeks spoke Greek, Bulgarians spoke Bulgarian, Arabs spoke Arabic."

The Ottoman state was based on Islamic principles, not nationalism. The Sultan's non-Muslim subjects were divided according to religion into a *millet* system that allowed minorities to control their own affairs, such as education, welfare, and civil law. While legally inferior to Muslims and under a heavier tax burden in lieu of performing military

Atatürk, proclaimed the Republic of Turkey from what remained of the non-Arab lands of the former Ottoman Empire.[266] Traumatized by the slow collapse of the multi-ethnic Ottoman empire, a demise accelerated by the nationalism of the Sultan's Christian subjects and the meddling of the great powers, the new state countered with its own brand of nationalism: "In the circumstances, the need for self-assertion among the Turkish, Sunni majority following the collapse of the Ottoman empire and the struggle to free Turkey from occupying powers proved paramount."[267]

Consequently, the many different ethnic groups living in the newly-founded Republic of Turkey were to be subsumed voluntarily or by force into a new Turkish national and linguistic identity that, while open to all, would broach no competitors.[268] For the founders of the new Turkish Republic, the Treaty of Lausanne once and for all ended the "minorities question" by dividing the population into three non-Muslim minorities enjoying minority rights and a Muslim—soon to be Turkish—majority.[269] One scholar has noted that,

---

service, Christians and Jews, as so-called "People of the Book," (*dhimmis*), were afforded religious and other protections. See, Justin McCarthy, *The Ottoman Turks* (London and New York: Longman), especially pp. 106-8, 127-31, and 205-6.

[266]The genesis of a new state can be found in the National Pact (*Misak-I Millî*), adopted in January 1920. That document, among other things, called for an indivisible state for the "Ottoman Muslim majority." The fate of territories having an Arab majority would be decided by plebiscite. With the exception of the oil-rich Mosul province, the Republic of Turkey fits largely in the borders envisioned by the National Pact. Zürcher, pp. 143-4.

[267]Andrews, p. 35.

[268]The only exception, of course, would be the non-Muslim minorities (Greek, Jewish, Armenian) given special linguistic and cultural rights under the 1923 Treaty of Lausanne.

[269]Signed on July 23, 1923, with the major Allied Powers of World War I, the Treaty of Lausanne recognized the new state created in what Turks call, "The War of National Liberation," a four-year struggle led by Mustafa Kemal, Atatürk. Among other things, the treaty envisioned a population exchange between Greece and Turkey, whereby the majority of Turks in Greece and the majority of Greeks in Turkey would move to their nominal country of origin. The treaty, however, allowed the Greeks of Istanbul and the Turks of Western Thrace to remain in their homes and granted them certain linguistic, cultural, and religious rights outlined in Articles 37-45 of the treaty. Consequently, the Turkish state acknowledged no minorities aside from the non-Muslim minorities (Greeks, Jews, and Armenians) mentioned in the treaty.

An official explanation of Article 81 of the Political Party Law, which is titled "Preventing the Creation of Minorities," states that, "Aside from those minorities recognized in the Treaty of Lausanne, there are no minorities in our country. In a particular country, the

Soon after the establishment of the Republic of Turkey, its
government embarked upon a radical program of nation-
building. Ethnic diversity was perceived as a danger to the
integrity of the state, and the Kurds, as the largest non-Turkish
ethnic group, obviously constituted the most serious threat. They
were decreed to be Turks, and their language and culture were
to be Turkish. All external symbols of their ethnic identity were
suppressed....There was no official discrimination against those
Kurds who agreed to be assimilated: they could reach the highest
positions in the state apparatus. Those who refused, however,
often met with severe repression.[270]

The use of Kurdish—along with other languages—was prohibited in
teaching as was its public use.[271] By 1930, publishing in languages other than
Turkish was prohibited by an act of parliament that was heralded under the slogan
of "Citizen, Speak Turkish!" (*Vatandaş, Türkçe Konuş!*).[272] The Kurdish names of
towns and villages in southeastern Turkey were also changed to Turkish.[273]

In time, the architects of the new Turkish nation-state began to deny
outright the existence of other ethnicities, especially Kurds, and attempted to create
murky Turkish genealogies for them.[274] Visions of a new civic nationalism based

---

knowledge of some languages other than the official one or [the fact of those languages]
being spoken from place to place does not create a minority." See Osman Selim
Kocahanoğlu, *Gerekçeli Siyasi Partiler ve Seçim Mevzuatı (Annotated Political Parties and
Election Body of Laws)*, (Istanbul:Temel Yayınları, 1994), p. 68.

[270]Van Bruinessen, p. 619.

[271]Zürcher, p. 178.

[272]Andrews, p. 34. The banning of Kurdish as a language of publication occurred
almost at the same time as the switch to a modified Latin alphabet. Parliament passed a law
to that effect on November 1, 1928, to be implemented as of January 1, 1929. According to
the 1927 census, the literacy rate in Turkey was 9 percent. See Ahmad, p. 81.

[273] Article 2/d/2 of the 1949 Provincial Administration Law No. 5442 (İl Idaresi
Kanunu) was amended in 1959 to state that, "Village names that are not Turkish and give
rise to confusion are to be changed in the shortest possible time by the Interior Ministry after
receiving the opinion of the Provincial Permanent Committee."

[274]For a good accounting of this process, see Kirişci and Winroth, pp. 102-108.
The authors argue that, "...In the 1930s great efforts were expended to prove that Kurds were
Turks... according to this, Kurds were comprised of Turks who to a great extent had changed
their language..."

Oddly enough, all three Turkish constitutions have conspicuously avoided linking

on social traits transmitted by education rather than on "consanguinity"degenerated into a rigid ethno-nationalism.[275] While there was no outright discrimination based on ethnicity, the lines between Turkish ethnicity and nationality began to be blurred beyond distinction.[276] A leading analyst of Turkey writes that, "The Kurds were relegated to the status of 'mountain Turks.' The denial of identity went to absurd lengths. In case a Turkish soldier should hear the word Kurd mentioned while on duty in the southeast, his service handbook informed him that this was a nickname born of the 'kürt, kürt' sound made when crunching through the 'mountain Turkish' snow."[277]

Blanket denial of ethnic identity—a reaction to the reemergence in the 1960s and 1970s of public expressions of Kurdish ethnic identity—reached a high

---

Turkish ethnicity with citizenship. Article 88 of the 1924 Constitution stated that, "In Turkey, from the point of view of citizenship, everyone is a Turk without regard to race or religion." Article 54 of the 1961 Constitution stated that, "Every individual who is bound to the Turkish state by ties of citizenship is a Turk." Article 66 of the present constitution, adopted in 1982, states that, "Everyone bound to the Turkish State through the bond of citizenship is a Turk."

[275]The early authors of Turkish nationalism envisioned no iron link between Turkish ethnicity and Turkish nationalism, i.e. citizenship in the Republic of Turkey. In his 1920 work *The Principles of Türkism*, Ziya Gökalp, the father of modern Turkish nationalism, wrote that,

...since race has no relationship to social traits, neither can it have any with nationality, which is the sum total of social characteristics...social solidarity rests on cultural unity, which is transmitted by means of education and therefore has no relationship with consanguinity...a nation is not a racial or ethnic or geographic or political or volitional group but one composed of individuals who share a common language, religion, morality, or aesthetics, that is to say, who have received the same education.

See Ziya Gökalp, *The Principles of Turkism* (Ankara, 1920, translated by Robert Devereux, Leiden, 1968), pp. 12-15 as quoted by David McDowall, *A Modern History of the Kurds* (London: I.B. Taurus, 1996), p. 189.

In fact, Gökalp was himself most likely a Kurd, born and raised in Diyarbakır.

[276]At the time, some saw the logical contradiction in using the identity of a specific ethnic group (Turks) as the national identity in a multi-ethnic republic. A short-lived "Anatolian" movement sought to adopt the geographic term "Anatolia" and "Anatolian" in place of "Turkey and "Turks." See Andrews, p. 35.

[277]Kurd in Turkish is spelled "Kürt." Hugh and Nicole Pope, "Turkey Unveiled: Atatürk and After." (London: John Murray, 1997), pp. 251-2.

The author of this report was told a similar story in 1987 by a Turkish friend who had completed military service in 1984 near Erzincan, a mixed Turkish-Kurdish area.

point after the military coup of 1980. A month before the military relinquished power in the elections of November 1983, Law No. 2932, "The Law Concerning Publications and Broadcasts in Languages Other Than Turkish," was passed. It declared that "The mother tongue of all Turkish citizens is Turkish " and, defying anthropology, forbade the use of any language but Turkish "as a mother tongue." It also prohibited all publishing in Kurdish.

Today, the situation concerning ethnic identity and language use has improved compared with the past. The late President Turgut Özal, himself of partial Kurdish origin, did much to break down the taboos concerning Kurds. In 1991, he successfully pushed to lift Law No. 2932 to permit publishing in Kurdish. The collapse of the USSR, which allowed the non-Kurdish ethnic minorities of Turkey such as Chechens and Circassians to reestablish links with relatives in the former Soviet Union, also helped break down the official doctrine of monoethnicity.[278] Kurds now speak their native tongue throughout the country without the ineffective and absurd legal prohibitions of Law No. 2932, and Kurdish music and videos are widely available and played openly, including in the conflict region in southeastern Turkey.[279] The so-called "Kurdish question" is discussed in the press, and in July 1995, for the first time, a survey was conducted among Kurds regarding their attitudes toward the PKK and an independent Kurdish state.[280] In 1994 and 1995, the leader of the New Democracy Movement (YDH), Cem Boyner, made full cultural and linguistic rights for Kurds a major part of his platform. Finally, some limited radio broadcasting in Kurdish, although still prohibited by

---

[278]Ethnic conflict in the former Soviet Union, especially in Abkhazia and Chechnya, also helped to strengthen ethnic sentiment among non-Turks in Turkey. See a series that ran in the now-closed newspaper Güneş (Istanbul), "Öbür denizin çocukları ya da Adığler" (The Children of the other Sea, or Adygei"), August 22, 1990. One of those interviewed refers to himself as an "assimilated Circassian." See also a piece about the war in Abkhazia, Nebil Özgentürk, "Kafdağının etekleri: Abhazya" ("The foothills of Caucasus Mountains: Abkhazia"), Sabah (Istanbul), October 4, 1992, and also a thoughtful essay by Thomas Goltz on Circassians and Chechens in Turkey in the wake of conflict in Chechnya, "The Turkish Carpet Frays," The Washington Post, January 28, 1996, p. C2. In the spring of 1995, the intellectual journal Birikim devoted a whole issue to ethnic minorities in Turkey, Etnik Kimlik ve Azınlıklar (Ethnic Identity and Minorities), No. 71-2, March-April 1995.

[279]Several Kurdish-language music videos were played on inter-city buses while the author of this report was traveling in southeastern Turkey in the summer of 1997.

[280]Doğu Sorunu: Teşhisler ve Tesbitler (The Eastern Question: Diagnosis and Ascertations), TOBB, July 1995. The report was sponsored by the Turkish Chamber of Commerce and written by Professor Doğu Ergil.

law, is taking place, and there appear to be plans to allow some sort of Kurdish-language television.

Despite these improvements, serious problems remain. The constitution, Political Parties Law, the Law Concerning the Founding and Broadcasts of Television and Radio, the Foreign Language Education and Teaching Law, and the Law Concerning Fundamental Provisions on Elections and Voter Registries Provincial Administration Law, all prohibit or restrict with certain exceptions the use of languages other than Turkish. Political parties are still banned for "creating minorities" if they demand linguistic and cultural rights for Kurds. A recent attempt by a private foundation to teach Kurdish ran head-first into a legal brick wall. Broadcasting in Kurdish and other non-Turkish languages spoken as a mother tongue by citizens of Turkey is still prohibited by law. While publishing in Kurdish and other languages is legally unrestricted, the constitutional basis for such prohibitions remains.

Şefik Beyaz, the head of the unregistered Kurdish Institute, joked that, "The authorities will not allow us to have a sign that says Kurdish Institute or to register as such, but when the police call they say, 'Is this the Kurdish Institute?"[281] Şeraffettin Elçi, an ethnic Kurd and former public works minister, summed up the situation by stating that,

> When I was a minister and said in public I was a Kurd, the whole society was shaken. It was treated as a manifesto. The whole state was in turmoil, and I was punished under Article 142. Now when someone says he is a Kurd there is no reaction. Things have changed, but this doesn't mean that "Kurdishness" has a legal status.[282]

---

[281]Interview, Istanbul, August 1997. In 1991, a group of individuals tried to register officially as the Sheik Said Foundation, in honor of a Kurdish tribal leader who led a revolt in 1925. When that request was rejected, they tried again in 1994 as the "Kurdish Institute." According to Mr. Beyaz, the court rejected the new name under Article 34b of a secret National Security Council directive (*MGK genelgesi*). The contents of the directive were not revealed to Mr. Beyaz or his lawyer. Undeterred, they founded the Mesopotamian Printing and Publishing Limited Company (Mezopotamya Basın ve Yayın A.Ş.).

[282]Interview, Ankara, August 1997. He is presently the leader of the Democratic Mass Party (*DKP*). In April 1979, Mr. Elçi stated in parliament that, "There are Kurds in Turkey. I am a Kurd." Article 142, now abolished, criminalized a number of actions, including conducting "propaganda with the purpose of establishing the domination of one social class over another..or to eliminate or weaken nationalist feelings..."

In Education

Under Article 42.9 of the constitution, Turkish is the official—though not exclusive—language of instruction.[283] In fact, the country's two most elite universities, the Middle East Technical University (ODTÜ) and Bosphorous University (Boğaziçi), use English as the language of instruction; the most elite high school, Galatasary Lisesi, uses French. Article 2a of Law No. 2923, the Foreign Language Education and Teaching Law, passed in October 1983, regulates the teaching of foreign languages, "taking into consideration the view of the National Security Council." In short, the National Security Council per decree decides which foreign languages may be taught in Turkey. At present, the following foreign languages can be taught in public and private learning institutions: English, French, German, Russian, Italian, Spanish, Arabic, Japanese, and Chinese.[284]

Consequently, state officials have blocked efforts to provide Kurdish-language instruction. While education in Kurdish takes place in informal settings and through tutors, such actions are, strictly speaking, illegal. A legally-registered foundation, however, the Kurdish Cultural and Research Foundation (Kürt-Kav), has been fighting a two-year battle to provide Kurdish language instruction at its headquarters in Istanbul. The foundation is the first organization in Turkey to have

---

[283] Article 42.9 states that, "No language other than Turkish shall be taught as a mother tongue to Turkish citizens at any institution of training or education." The Treaty of Lausanne, however, allows instruction in Greek and Armenian, and the constitution recognizes this provision.

[284] Decision No. 92/2788, *Official Gazette*, March 20, 1992. Oddly enough, the now-abolished Law No. 2932, "The Law Concerning Publications and Broadcasts in Languages Other than Turkish," was more liberal regarding teaching foreign languages. Article 2 of that law stated that, " Apart from the first official language of states recognized by the Turkish State, the release, propagation, or publication of thoughts in any other language is prohibited."

the legal right to use the term "Kurdish" in its title. [285] Yılmaz Çamlıbel, the chairman of Kürt-Kav, complained that,

> In August 1996, we applied to the Istanbul Governor's office to teach courses in Kurdish. This request was forwarded to the Education Ministry, which requested us to bring various documents. On March 20, 1997, we were denied the right to teach Kurdish courses under the Foreign Language Education and Teaching Law No. 2923. [286]

The Ministry of Education defended its decision by citing Law No. 2923: "In the Council of Minister's decision number 92/2783 published in the Official Gazette no. 21177 of 20.03.92, the languages of instruction and education in official and private courses in Turkey have been determined to be English, French, German, Russian, Italian, Spanish, Arabic, Japanese, and Turkish. Because of this, the opening of courses outside of those listed is not possible because of the present body of law in force." [287]

As a result of the ruling, in June 1997, police sealed the floor of the foundation where the classes were to be held. A case was opened at the request of the Ministry of Education against Mr. Çamlıbel and his aide, Mehmet Celal Baykara, for "opening a course illegally." In May 1998, the court acquitted both men of the charge, but ruled that the foundation could not hold Kurdish language courses. [288]

---

[285] The official name of the foundation in Kurdish and Turkish is *Weqfa Lêkolin û Çanda Kurdi/ Kürt Kültür ve Araştırma Vakfı*. After a four-year legal battle, the foundation won the right to use the word "Kurdish" in its official title in a January 16, 1996, decision by the High Appeals Court (*Yargıtay*).

A Kürt-Kav member explained that, "We founded our institute in 1992, ninety-eight of us. We are not ideological—our goal is to build civil society by studying and teaching the Kurdish culture and language. It took us four years of struggle to get the right to have the name 'Kurdish' in our title." According to Kürt-Kav's statute, its main goal is "research on fundamental rights and freedoms (and) research and investigation in the areas of the Kurdish language, culture, and history."

[286] Interview, Istanbul, August 1997.

[287] T.C. Milli Eğitim Bakanlığı Hukuk Müşavirliği (Republic of Turkey, Ministry of Education, Legal Department), Correspondence No. 97-200=11=897=12586.

[288] "Turk Court Acquits Two in Kurdish Courses Case," Reuters, May 5, 1998. Ironically, the Istanbul State Security Court uses Kürt-Kav to provide transcription and translation of Kurdish-language documents.

For its part, Kürt-Kav appealed the Ministry of Education's decision, but an administrative court rejected its claim on November 12, 1997. The foundation has subsequently filed an appeal with a higher court, where the case is now pending.

Efforts to teach Turkish in rural areas where ethnic Kurds predominate have had mixed results. In a recent interview, Dr. Salih Yıldırım, the state minister responsible for southeastern Turkey, stated that one-third of those living in the region did not speak Turkish, a figure that rose to 50 percent among women.[289] In practical terms, the inability to communicate often causes problems when dealing with state authorities, especially in attempts to access services like health care.[290] The inability to speak Turkish among rural Kurds is a legacy of underdevelopment and poverty, traditional family structure, and, more recently, the conflict in the region. The PKK has a policy of assassinating teachers, while many schools have been abandoned as a result of the government's counterinsurgency campaign.

Some argue that restrictions on the "teaching of a mother tongue" other than Turkish should be removed and that private instruction in Kurdish should be allowed. Professor Bülent Tanör, a constitutional scholar at Istanbul University, stated that,

> In Turkey it is okay to have Turkish as the official language. But what the mother tongue is is a different matter. This raises two problems. Kurdish education in the state system and outside the state system. There are foundations outside the state system, like

---

[289]Neşe Düzel, "Pazartesi Konuşmaları" ("Monday Chats"), *Yeni Yüzyıl* (Istanbul), Internet edition, April 27, 1997. Dr. Yıldırım also stated that 61 percent of women in the region were illiterate.

In a ground breaking survey of Turkish Kurds released in 1995, 68.5 percent stated that they spoke Kurdish at home, while 15.1 percent reported speaking Turkish and 14.2 percent stated that they spoke both Turkish and Kurdish. The sample consisted of 1,267 individuals (Diyarbakır, 237; Batman, 188; Mardin, 219; Adana, 188; Mersin, 185; Antalya, 250). See, *Doğu Sorunu*, pp. 12-13.

[290]According to a report put out by the Turkish Medical Association (Türk Tabipleri Birliği), half of the doctors working at health facilities in Diyarbakır needed a third person to communicate with patients. Sixty-seven percent of midwives and nurses stated that they had language problems even when administering simple procedures, like vaccinations. See, Turkish Medical Association, *The Report on the Health Services and Health Personnel Problems in the Southeast*, Ankara, March 1995, pp. 44-48.

Kurt-Kav, but they face problems. These problems could be solved.[291]

In a study on democratization for the Turkish Industrialists and Businessmens' Association (TÜSİAD), Mr. Tanör wrote that,

> The...Foreign Language Education and Teaching Law...is very strange: "The mother tongue of the Turkish citizens cannot be taught in any language other than Turkish (2923-14.10.1983 Article 2/a)." The element of strangeness is...[that] according to the meaning of the sentence, it is possible for a Turkish citizen to have a mother tongue other than Turkish, but that mother tongue can be taught only in Turkish....the last paragraph of Article 42 of the constitution which rejects a natural and social phenomenon as the "mother tongue" and treats it as an official language is disturbing, even offensive. There is absolutely no need for this. The state, the constitution, and the laws have the right to decree that the official language be taught as the primary and mandatory language in all schools. But the expression of this should in no way be like the one in the stated provisions....It is also useful to mention...the Convention on the Rights of the Child, which Turkey has ratified with reservations. [It] states that....States...agree that the education of the child shall be directed to...development of respect for the child's parents, his or her own cultural identity, language and values....[292]

For their part, a majority of ethnic Kurds polled wanted the right to decide what the language of instruction should be for their children.[293]

---

[291]Interview, Istanbul, August 1997.

[292]*Perspectives on Democratization in* Turkey, pp. 172-4.

[293]According to the survey, 60.1 percent believed that every ethnic group should be able to obtain an education in its native tongue if its members so chose. 12.6 percent preferred Turkish language instruction, while 3.6 percent wanted only Kurdish. Economic realities, however, played a role. Most acknowledged that neither Turkish nor Kurdish would be sufficient as a language in the global economy. This view was summed up in the phrase, "If the prohibition is removed, very few would send their children to Kurdish schools. Would they let their kids be unemployed?" See *Doğu Sorunu*, pp. 43-44.

In Politics

Prohibitions concerning the use of minority languages—together with general restrictions concerning the discussion of minorities—extend to politics. The use of languages other than Turkish in political campaigns is forbidden by law. Additionally, a general prohibition exists against parties that claim that there are minorities based, "on national, religious, confessional, racial, or language differences." While these restrictions do not specify Kurds or the use of Kurdish, they are, de facto, the main target. Article 81 of the 1983 Political Parties Law (No. 2820), "Preventing the Creation of Minorities," states that,

> Political parties:
>
> a) cannot put forward that minorities based on national, religious, confessional, racial, or language differences exist in the Republic of Turkey.
>
> b) cannot advocate the goal of destroying national unity or be engaged in activities to this end; by means of protecting, developing, or disseminating language or cultures other than the Turkish language and culture and thus create minorities in the Republic of Turkey.
>
> c) cannot use a language other than Turkish in writing and printing party statutes or programs, at congresses, indoors or outside; at demonstrations, and in propaganda; cannot use or distribute placards, pictures, phonograph records, voice and visual tapes, brochures and statements written in a language other than Turkish; cannot remain indifferent to these actions and acts committed by others. However, it is possible to translate party statutes and programs into foreign languages other than those forbidden by law.[294]

---

[294]*Political Parties Law/ Siyasi Partiler Kanunu* (No. 2820, adopted April 26, 1983) in Kocahanoğlu, p. 68 and pp. 100-101.

Part Four of the *Political Parties Law* deals with, "Prohibitions concerning Political Parties." It is divided into Section One (Article 78), "Prohibitions concerning Goals and Activities" and Section Two (Articles 79-83), "Defending the Qualities of the Nation-State."

The election law reinforces the prohibition on the use of languages other than Turkish. Article 58 states that, "....It is forbidden to use any other language or script than Turkish in propaganda disseminated in radio or television as well as in other election propaganda."[295]

. Article 81 of the Political Parties Law and associated legislation has hindered discussion of the Kurdish question in the political arena and has led to the banning of several non-violent political parties that advocated increased cultural or linguistic rights for ethnic Kurds.[296] In the 1991 general elections, one of the

---

[295]*The Law Concerning Fundamental Provisions on Elections and Voter Registries/ Seçimlerin Temel Hükümleri ve Seçmen Kütükleri Hakkında Kanun* (No. 298, Adopted April 26, 1961), reprinted by State authority Kocahanoğlu, pp. 252-253.

[296] Banned parties include the following: Socialist Party (Sosyalist Partisi-SP), October 25, 1992; People's Labor Party (Halkın Emek Partisi-HEP), July 14, 1993; Freedom and Democracy Party (Özgürlük ve Demokrasi Partisi-ÖZDEP), November 23, 1993; Democracy Party (Demokrasi Partisi-DEP), June 30, 1994; Socialist Union Party (Sosyalist Birlik Partisi-SBP), July 19, 1995; Democracy and Change Party (Değisim ve Demokrasi Partisi-DDP), 1996.

HEP, ÖZDEP, DEP, and the present People's Democracy Party (*Halkın Demokrasi Partisi-HADEP*), are continuations of each other. Each new party was formed as the previous one was closed by the Constitutional Court.

In addition, members of these parties often faced criminal proceedings for free expression that is protected under international law. In December 1994, eight former DEP parliamentarians were convicted "of being members of an outlawed armed group" and "aiding and abetting" such a group in a trial fraught with procedural irregularities. Four are still imprisoned. All have appealed their case to the European Court of Human Rights in Strasbourg.

Unless otherwise noted, information in this paragraph comes from the annual reports of the Human Rights Foundation of Turkey (*Türkiye İnsan Hakları Vakfı-TİHV*). See *1992 Türkiye İnsan Hakları Raporu (1992 Turkey Human Rights Report)*, (Ankara: Human Rights Foundation of Turkey, January 1993), pp. 189-99; *1993 Türkiye İnsan Hakları Raporu (1993 Turkey Human Rights Report)*, (Ankara: Human Rights Foundation of Turkey, June 1994), pp. 303-5; *1994 Turkey Human Rights Report* (Ankara: Human Rights Foundation of Turkey, September 1995), pp. 348-355; *1995 Türkiye İnsan Hakları Raporu (1995 Turkey Human Rights Report)*, (Ankara: Human Rights Foundation of Turkey, February 1997), pp. 394-406.

banned parties, the People's Labor Party (HEP), won twenty-two seats in parliament.[297] A leading constitutional scholar commented that,

> As a legal scholar, the main point in the Kurdish question is to remove Article 81 from the Political Parties Law. Parties advocating Kurdish identity should be allowed to operate. This will provide some breathing space to Turkish politics and make the Kurds more part of the Turkish establishment. The biggest obstacle to achieving this is chauvinism and fear. If you can get rid of Article 81, you can get a breath of fresh air. Even if Article 81 is lifted, there will still be other actions that forbid separatist activity that are based in international law.[298]

Presently, the Democratic Mass Party *(Demokrat Kitle Partisi-*DKP) of Şeraffettin Elçi faces closure under Article 81 of the Political Parties 'Law and associated legislation.[299] The DKP advocates cultural and linguistic rights for all minorities and the decentralization of administration within Turkey's present

---

[297]In 1991, in an election alliance with the Social Democratic Populist Party *(Sosyal Demokrat Halkçı Parti-SHP)*, twenty-two HEP parliamentarians were elected from the HEP-SHP list, all from southeastern Turkey. HEP was formed in 1990 after six ethnic Kurdish deputies from SHP were ejected from the party for attending an October 1989 conference in Paris titled, "Kurds: Human Rights and Cultural Identity." The Kurdish Institute of Paris sponsored the conference.

When HEP was closed eighteen former deputies joined DEP. When DEP was closed it had thirteen deputies in Parliament; eight, as mentioned, were put on trial, and five fled abroad. HADEP, DEP's successor, contested the December 1995 parliamentary elections and won 4.5 percent of the vote, but could not pass the 10 percent parliamentary barrier.

[298]Interview with Bülent Tanör, Istanbul, August 1997. In his report for TÜSİAD, Mr. Tanör wrote that, "The provisions of this article (Article 81) are dramatic from the point of respect for logic and culture....The democratic and rational approach requires that political parties seeking to represent different ethnic and religious identities, on the condition that they are not separatist, should not be excluded from the system but included." See *Perspectives on Democratization*, pp. 45-46.

[299]*Iddianame*, (Indictment), SP.91 Hz.1997/138. The prosecutor alleges that the party has violated the preamble and Articles 2 ,3, 14, 68, and 136 of the constitution as well as Articles 78, 80, 81, and 89 of the Political Parties Law. See pp. 72-3.

borders.[300] In June 1997, the state prosecutor filed a seventy-three page indictment with the Constitutional Court to close the DKP and ban Mr. Elçi from politics for five years because of the party's program and various press statements made by Mr. Elçi.

The state prosecutor cited the statements below as reasons to close the party:

•   "As a participatory, liberal, and democratic mass party that, together with solving all the country's problems, places a peaceful and democratic solution of the Kurdish question at the center of its program, the Democratic Mass Party strives to restructure the state and institute a democracy in the country with all its rules and institutions....Kurds, like Turks, are a fundamental element of this country. Within Turkey's unity and political borders...they want to live in peace and brotherhood....It is impossible to solve the Kurdish question by resorting to violence or repression" (Party Program).[301]

•   "We use democratic and peaceful methods. As the Kurdistan Workers Party, the PKK entered political life; we do not approve of their actions" (Statement to *Cumhuriyet,* Istanbul daily).[302]

---

[300]Mr. Elçi complained that,

In Europe, there is a new movement: protecting regionalism, protecting difference, but then joining together. Look at Spain and Catalonia....There has been a serious change in the world. The bipolar world is over. The European Union gives importance to minorities and to regional differences. Whether Turkey wants to or not they are affected....The benefit of closing our party is not understandable by rationality. Powers in the state want a hard-line approach....[there is] a paradox about the state fighting the PKK. If they were serious, they would not interfere with democratic, non-violent movements like ours that defend the unity of the state...the state doesn't want the voice of Kurds to be raised even in a peaceful, western fashion it seems.

Interview, Ankara, September 1997.

[301]*Demokratik Kitle Partisi Programı* (Program of the Democratic Mass Party), pp. 3 and 32-3. Cited in the indictment, pp. 5 and 8-9. SP.91 Hz.1997/138 as pp. 3 and 32-3.

[302]"Elçi'den eyalet çözümü" ("Decentralization solution from Elçi"), *Cumhuriyet,* January 4, 1997, p. 5, cited in the indictment, SP.91 Hz.1997/138, p. 15.

- "....We say that injustices done to the Kurds must be rectified. As the President stated in 1992, 'the Kurdish reality' must be recognized. It must be recognized and legal protection must be given to the fact that Kurds are also a fundamental element in this society" (Interview with Şahin Alpay, *Milliyet*).[303]

The indictment against the DKP shows both the progress Turkey has made in acknowledging the existence of minorities as well as the great distance the country must still travel to make that recognition a working and meaningful proposition. The prosecutor does not argue that Kurds or other minorities do not exist. On the contrary, he states that such groups actually enrich society as a whole as long as they keep their activities at the level of the individual, and not demand group rights. The prosecutor argues that,

The State is neutral and disinterested regarding the origins of individuals' lineages. There is no obstacle against anyone, including those of Kurdish ethnicity, from expressing his own identity. In fact, cultural identities and differences are elements that enrich a common culture based on social solidarity, experiences, honored judgements, unity (*birliktelik*), social life and a common past. In that respect, Article 81 of the Political Parties Law does not forbid individuals that constitute the [Turkish] nation from expressing different languages and cultures and ethnic differences. *However, the necessary point that must be stressed and pointed out is that expressing identities must be done without claiming that one is a member of a minority or a member of a nation and within the spirit and knowledge that one is a member of the egalitarian and unifying wholeness of the Turkish Nation and its totality.* There are no prohibited languages in Turkey today. Aside from public (*kamusal*) affairs, every citizen can use the language of his

---

[303]"Geleceğe umutla bakıyorum," ("I'm Positive About the Future"), *Milliyet*, February 10, 1997, cited in the indictment, SP.91 Hz.1997/138, p. 18.

On December 8, 1991, while on a trip to southeastern Turkey with his coalition partner and deputy prime minister, Erdal İnönü, the newly-elected prime minister, Suleyman Demirel, announced that "Turkey had recognized the Kurdish reality." See Düzgören, pp. 123-4.

choice in private life, for example books, newspapers, journals, and music cassettes can be produced in the Kurdish language.[304]

The election law prohibits the use of "languages" other than Turkish, which in effect targets Kurdish. Article 58 of the *Law Concerning Fundamental Provisions on Elections and Voter Registries* states that, "....It is forbidden to use any other language or script than Turkish in propaganda disseminated in radio or television as well as in other election propaganda."[305]

Mr. Nurettin Basut, who ran as an independent candidate during the 1991 parliamentary elections and on the HADEP list in the 1995 general elections, faced prosecution under Article 58 of the Election Law both times for speaking Kurdish. According to the indictment in the second case, Mr. Basut and another suspect in the case "spoke Kurdish at a rally organized by HADEP in Ağrı province and [thereby] acted contradictory to the prohibitions outlined in Article 58 of Law No. 298..."[306] Both men were found guilty and given seven-month sentences. This conviction superseded a one-year, four-month suspended sentence Mr. Basut received in the case stemming from the 1991 elections. He has appealed the second case, which is still pending.

In Broadcasting

Prohibitions still prevent the use of Kurdish in broadcasting. The abolition of Law No. 2932 of October 1983 ("The Law Concerning Publications and Broadcasts in Languages Other Than Turkish") removed legal obstacles to publishing in Kurdish and other languages, but not impediments to broadcasting.[307]

---

[304] Indictment, SP.91 Hz.1997/138, p. 68. Italics added. The prosecutor is in error by stating that there are no prohibited languages. Restrictions still exist in broadcasting and education.

[305] *Seçimlerin Temel Hükümleri ve Seçmen Kütükleri Hakkında Kanun* (no. 298, adopted April 26, 1961), reprinted in Kocahanoğlu, pp. 252-53.

[306] T.C. Ağrı Cumhuriyet Başsavcılığı, Iddianame, (Republic of Turkey, Ağrı Republic Head Prosecution Office, Indictment), No. 1996/9, January 11, 1996.

Interview with Mr. Basut, Istanbul, August 1997.

[307] Article 2 of the law, for example, stated that, "Aside from the first official language of states recognized by the Turkish State, the announcing, disseminating, or publishing of thoughts in any language is forbidden." Article 3a stated that, "The use of any language but Turkish as a mother tongue or being engaged in any type of activity of its dissemination is forbidden." Article 23e of the Anti-Terror Law (No. 3713), passed on April 12, 1991, abolished Law No. 2932.

The constitutional basis for Law No. 2932, however, still exists.[308] The 1994 RTÜK law, which regulates radio and television broadcasting, mandates the exclusive use of Turkish except in certain circumstances.[309]

Despite an absolute prohibition against broadcasting in Kurdish, Kurdish-language music and music videos—as long as they are not overtly political—seem to be tolerated. The army, in fact, runs a radio station called "Voice of the Tigris" (*Dicle Radyosu*) that broadcasts in the two major Kurdish dialects, Kurmancı and Sorani, as well as in Turkish and Turkmen. An observer of the Kurds in Turkey commented that, "Kurdish music is played, as long as it is not political. And there are music videos in Kurdish, some shot in Northern Iraq and some in Europe....There are no talk shows in Kurdish, however."[310] Dr. Haluk Şahin, the news coordinator at *Kanal D,* a mainstream private television station, noted that, "There are stories from the region [ethnic Kurdish areas of southeastern Turkey], and people speak in Kurdish so we subtitle them in Turkish. Occasionally, people have sung songs in Kurdish."[311] Mustafa Altıoklar is planning to subtitle in Kurdish his film *Heavy Novel (Ağır Roman)*, a bleak depiction of poverty and police abuse in Istanbul.[312] Those who have tried to do more, however, have faced serious obstacles.[313]

---

[308]Article 28.2 of the constitution states that, "Publication shall not be made in any language prohibited by law...."
Article 26 states that,

> No language prohibited by law shall be used in the expression and dissemination of thought. Any written or printed documents, phonograph records, magnetic or video tapes, and other means of expression used in contravention of this provision shall be seized by a duly issued decision of a judge or, in cases where delay is deemed prejudicial, by the competent authority designated by law.

[309]Article 4t of the RTÜK Law, "Broadcasting Principles," states that, "Radio and television broadcasts will be made in Turkish; however, for the purpose of teaching or of imparting news those foreign languages that have made a contribution to the development of universal cultural and scientific works can be used." See Appendix for a text of the law.
State television has nightly newscasts in English, German, and French, and any number of foreign language channels are available through cable television.

[310]Interview with Koray Düzgören, Istanbul, August 1997.

[311]Interview, Istanbul, August 1997.

[312]Yalman Onaran, *A Heavy Film*, Associated Press, January 31, 1998.

[313]Nevzat Bingöl operated the first television station that broadcast both music and political programming in Kurdish. Based in Diyarbakır, the station closed in 1997 under both political and economic pressure. See Amberin Zaman, "Kurdish Broadcasting," Voice

Many state officials realize the need to legalize Kurdish-language broadcasting given that many ethnic Kurds—especially those living in southeastern Turkey—speak Turkish poorly or not at all. Without such a medium, the state is unable to reach a substantial section of ethnic Kurds. Professor Doctor Salih Yıldırım, the state minister responsible for the southeast, recently commented that,

> Kurdish language television is necessary. Sixty-one percent of our women in the region are illiterate, and one-half do not know Turkish. If for the seventy-five year history of the republic you have not taught your people Turkish, you have not introduced your culture, do you have the right to hold someone responsible for that? If television stations like MED-TV presents its own fallacies and says they are correct, isn't the responsibility for this ours? There is nothing to be afraid of with Kurdish television. To explain your own facts to these people, you have to reach them in their own language, customs and usage, and traditions.[314]

Bülent Tanör, the legal scholar who authored the TÜSİAD report on democratization, echoed Professor Yıldırım's comments: "The military needs TV and radio in Kurdish to give its message. It sees that MED TV, which in effect is PKK TV, is effective. They [the military] have this "Tigris Radio" which broadcasts in Kurdish. It shows that the state recognizes that it has to do something."[315]

The prohibition on broadcasting in Kurdish prevents market forces from operating and thus short circuits Turkey's vibrant private sector. Restrictions raise transaction costs and make entry into prohibited areas attractive only to those ideologically committed or those able to flout the prohibition: in this case, a radio station operated by the Turkish Army and a satellite television station, MED TV

---

of America, July 31, 1998.

[314] "Pazartesi Konuşmaları" ("Monday Chats"), op. cit. In an August 1997 interview with Human Rights Watch, Dr. Hikmet Sami Türk, state minister for human rights, also expressed support for allowing Kurdish-language broadcasting.

Presently transmitting via satellite from the United Kingdom, MED-TV broadcasts several hours of programming a day overwhelmingly sympathetic to the PKK and its struggle. Many Kurds throughout Turkey watch MED as it represents the sole Kurdish-language television station available in Turkey.

[315] Interview, Istanbul, August 1997.

whose programming is largely sympathetic to the PKK and which regularly provides a forum for the PKK leader, Mr. Abdullah Öcalan. An ethnic Kurdish businessman from Diyarbakır commented that,

> You have to change the laws. If you don't change the laws, you can't do anything. It is because of the laws that there isn't Kurdish broadcasting. RTUK, other laws. The lack of Kurdish broadcasting is not a question of economics. Local businessmen would open Kurdish-language newspapers, radio stations, and television stations. It is natural, the case of meeting a demand in a capitalist economy. People would do market research. If there were no legal obstacles from the state, we would have a non-PKK Kurdish TV and more people would watch it than MED-TV. I would want MED-TV not to be the mouth of the PKK. I would want them to broadcast all parts of our people, it would be better.[316]

Publishing in Kurdish

Only a handful of small weekly newspapers or journals publish entirely or partly in Kurdish despite the absence of legal restrictions. None of the mainstream newspapers do. Oktay Ekşi, the head of Press Council of Turkey and chief columnist at the mass circulation daily *Hürriyet*, stated that lack of demand prevented his paper from publishing in Kurdish, even an insert or a single page. He argued that "Even they [those publishing in Kurdish] can't maintain their own newspapers."[317]

The Kurdish-language papers that do exist face legal pressure, but it is unclear whether such harassment is motivated by the content of the articles or the language in which they are written, or a combination of both. Koray Düzgören, a journalist who follows Kurdish issues, commented that, "The state doesn't discriminate. It wants to close Kurdish publications. Those that produce culture and literature survive to a greater extent."[318] Even the state minister for human rights, Dr. Hikmet Sami Türk, admitted that, "There are Kurdish-language newspapers,

---

[316]Interview, Diyarbakır, August 1997.

[317]Interview, August 1997, Istanbul. The logic behind the statement is that those most in need of a Kurdish-language paper, i.e. those with weak or non-existent Turkish, are usually illiterate in Kurdish and too poor to purchase a newspaper.

[318]Interview, Istanbul, August 1997.

but such repression against them, which does exist, shouldn't happen. But such newspapers do exist."[319]

The fate of the weekly, bilingual Turkish-Kurdish *Hêvi (Hope),* which started publishing in November 1996, is emblematic of the pressure that such publications face.[320] A majority of *Hêvi*'s weekly issues have been confiscated on the day of publication or shortly thereafter by state prosecutors, allegedly for violating Article 8 of the Anti-Terror Law or Article 312 of the penal code. The vast majority of confiscation orders are because of articles written in Turkish, not Kurdish. According to the paper's editor, Fehmi Işık,

> The paper is printed both abroad and within the country because of confiscations. Of the various issues of *Hevi,* only three to date have not been confiscated; the other thirty-six have been confiscated by DGM under Article 8 of the Anti-Terror Law or Article 312. Of all the issues we have published, in our various incarnations, only fifty were not confiscated. Confiscation decisions are strange. It is as if they don't even read the paper.[321]

Often criminal cases are opened in connection with the confiscation order. Mr. Işık added that, "At this point, in cases that have been confirmed by the appellate court, our responsible editor was sentenced to one year, six months and received a sentence of TL100 million (U.S. $624)." Other newspapers publishing in Kurdish have faced similar pressure.[322]

---

[319]Interview, Ankara, August 1997.

[320] The editorial policy of *Hêvi* is sympathetic to the Socialist Party of Kurdistan (*SPK*) of Kemal Burkay, presently a non-violent political party. The party is outlawed in Turkey, and its leader lives in exile.

[321]Interview, Istanbul, August 1997. Though not legally recognized as such, there have been various incarnations of the paper. Previous papers include the following: *Deng (Voice),* December 1989; *Azadi (Freedom),* 1991, published 104 issues then closed down by court order; *Deng Azadi* (Voice of Freedom), forty-two published, then closed; *Ronahi,* 1995, seventy-two published, closed.

[322]*Welat (Country),* was a Kurdish-language weekly that published 115 issues from 1992-94. The responsible editor of the publication, Mazhar Günbat, was sentenced in two different cases under Articles 312 and 8 of the Anti-Terror Law. He has since left Turkey, and the paper was closed by court order. Its successor, *Welatê Me (My Country),* which published forty-six issues in 1994 and 1995, also faced legal pressure. The paper's owner, Aynur Bozkurt, was fined TL100 million under Article 7 of the Anti-Terror Law, and the responsible editor, Mehmet Gemsiz, was sentenced to two years, six months under Article

Book publishing in Kurdish also seems to avoid legal prosecution when compared with Turkish-language publishing done by the same publishing house. Şefik Beyaz, the head of the unregistered Kurdish Institute, stated that, "Until today we have had four books confiscated. All were in Turkish. They try not to open a legal case against the ones in Kurdish."[323] Abdullah Keskin, the head of Avesta Publishing, commented that, "Our Kurdish-language books are not controversial. We publish poetry, novels, and stories. They don't confiscate these books...."[324] Since late 1996, the Mesopotamian Cultural Center (Mezopotamya Kültür Merkezi-MKM) has been publishing a monthly Kurdish-language arts journal, *Jiyana Rewşen*, which had escaped prosecution.[325]

Mr. Keskin, the head of Avesta Publishing, argued that, "The authorities don't confiscate these books because they don't want to recognize the Kurdish language." The lack of prosecutors and police officers who speak Kurdish may be another reason. Murat Batkı, the editor of *Jiyana Rewşen*, explained how he was asked by a prosecutor to provide a translation of an article for the prosecutor's investigation: "The prosecutor called me and said that he was thinking of opening a case against us but that he hadn't read any articles. He asked me to translate a few and bring them to him."[326] Most likely, both factors play a role.

---

312 and Article 7 of the Anti-Terror Law. He fled abroad as well, and the paper was closed. Since January 1996, the paper has been publishing under the name, Azadiya Welat (Free Country). As of January 1999, the publication was confiscated three times and there were five cases pending against it. In one of these cases, which ended on January 25, the court sentenced the responsible editor to one year of imprisonment and a 3 billion 50 million TL fine (U.S. $9298) and banned the publication of the paper for ten days. Azadiya Welat appealed the verdict. Interview with the paper's editor-in-chief, Sami Tan, Istanbul, August 1997; Interview with Azadiya Welat, January 1999.

[323]Interview, Istanbul, August 1997.
[324]Interview, Istanbul, November 1997.
[325]Through August 1997.
[326]Interview, Istanbul, August 1997.

X. APPENDIX

Excerpts from Relevant Laws and Decrees
(All translations unofficial.)
Constitution of the Republic of Turkey/Türkiye Cümhuriyeti Anayasası
(No. 2709, Adopted November 7, 1982)

Preamble, (Amended: 1995/4121.1)
(Paragraph 5)

> *No protection shall be given to thoughts or opinions that run counter to Turkish national interests, the fundamental principle of the existence of the indivisibility of the Turkish state and territory, the historical and moral values of Turkishness, or the nationalism, principles, reforms, and modernism of Atatürk, and that as required by the principle of secularism there shall be no absolutely no interference of sacred religious feeling in the affairs of state and politics;*

Article 4

> *The provisions of Article 1 of the constitution establishing the form of the state as a Republic, the provisions of Article 2 on the characteristics of the Republic, and the provisions of Article 3 shall not be amended, nor shall their amendment be proposed.*

Article 26—Freedom of Expression and the Dissemination of Thought

26.1 *Everyone has the right to express and disseminate his thought and opinion by speech, in writing, or in pictures or through other media, individually or collectively. This right includes the freedom to receive and impart information and ideas without interference from official authorities....*

26.2 *The exercise of these freedoms may be restricted for the purpose of preventing crime, punishing offenders, withholding information duly classified as a state secret, protecting the reputation and rights and the private and family life of others....*

26.3   *No language prohibited by law shall be used in the expression and dissemination of thought. Any written or printed documents, phonograph records, magnetic or video tapes, and other means of expression used in contravention of this provision shall be seized by a duly issued decision of a judge or, in cases where delay is deemed prejudicial, by the competent authority designated by law.*

Article 27—Freedom of Science and Arts

27.1   *Everyone has the right to study and teach freely, explain, disseminate science and arts and to carry out research in these fields.*

27.2   *The right to disseminate shall not be exercised for the purpose of changing the provisions of Articles 1, 2, 3, of this constitution....[327]*

Article 28—Freedom of the Press

28.1   *The press is free and shall not be censored. The establishment of a printing house shall not be subject to prior permission and to the deposit of financial guarantee.*

28.2   *Publication shall not be made in any language prohibited by law....*

28.4   *In the limitation of freedom of the press, Articles 26 and 27 of the constitution are applicable.*

28.5   *Anyone who writes or prints any news or articles which threaten the internal or external security of the state or the indivisible integrity of the state with its territory and nation, which tend to incite offense, riot or insurrection, or which refer to classified state secrets and anyone who prints or transmits such news or articles to others for the above purpose shall be held responsible under the law relevant to these offenses....*

---

[327]See Article 4.

Article 42.9

> *No language other than Turkish shall be taught as a mother tongue to Turkish citizens in teaching and learning institutions. Foreign languages to be taught at learning and teaching institutions and the rules under which schools conducting training and education in a foreign language are to be determined by law. The provisions of international treaties will be respected.*

Turkish Penal Code/ Türk Ceza Kanunu (No. 765, Adopted March 1, 1926)

Article 155

> *Those who, except in circumstances indicated in the aforementioned articles, publish articles inciting people to break the law or harm the security of the country, or make publications or suggestions that make people unwilling to serve in the military or make speeches to that end in public meetings or gathering places, shall be imprisoned from between two months to two years and be punished with a heavy fine of between twenty-five and 200 lira.*

> *N.B.: The monetary fine in the article written is raised 180 times.*

Article 158—(Amended: 1961/235)

> *Whoever insults the President of the Republic face-to-face or through cursing shall face a heavy penalty of not more than three years.*

> *If the insulting or cursing happens in the absence of the President of the Republic, those who commit the crime will be liable to imprisonment of between one and three years. Even if the name of the President of the Republic is not directly mentioned, allusion and hint shall be considered as an attack made directly against the President if there is presumptive evidence beyond a reasonable doubt that the attack was made against the President of Turkey.*

> *If the crime is committed in any published form, the punishment will increase from one-third to one-half.*

Article 159—(Amended:1961/235)

> *Those who publicly insult or ridicule the moral personality of Turkishness, the Republic, the Parliament, the Government, State Ministers, the military or security forces of the state, or the Judiciary will be punished with a penalty of no less than one year and no more than six years of maximum security imprisonment....*
>
> *If insulting Turkishness is carried out in a foreign country by a Turk the punishment given will be increased from one-third to one-half.*

Article 311—Inciting to commit a crime, Threatening with the goal of inciting panic and fear— (Amended: 1953/6123); (Amended: 1981/2370)

> *One who publicly incites the commission of a crime shall be punished in the ways below.*
>
> *1. If the penalty of the felony incited is higher than the duration of the heavy penalty, a heavy imprisonment of between three and five years;*
>
> *2. If limited heavy imprisonment or imprisonment is necessary, it will be from three months to three years imprisonment in accordance with the type of crime.*
>
> *3. In other circumstances, a heavy fine of between 1,000 and 5,000 lira will be applied.[328]*

(Amendment: 1981/2370)

> *If the incitement occurs by various means of mass media, sound tapes, records, films, papers, periodicals, or with other press instruments, or by writings written by hand and then multiplied and printed or distributed, or by signs or written announcements hung, the heavy imprisonment and fines which will be determined according to the paragraphs above will be doubled.*

---

[328]Fine later increased three times according to Turkish Penal Code Article 119.

Article 312--(Amended: 1981/2370)

> *One who openly praises an action considered criminal under the law or speaks positively about it or incites people to disobey the law shall be sentenced from six months to two years of imprisonment and to a heavy fine of between 2,000 and 10,000 lira.*[329]

> *One who openly incites people to enmity and hatred by pointing to class, racial, religious, confessional, or regional differences will be punished by imprisonment of between one to three years and a heavy fine of between 3,000 and 12,000 lira.*[330] *If the incitement is done in a way that could possibly be dangerous for public security, the punishment given to the perpetrator is increased from one-third to one-half.*

> *Penalties given to those who carry out crimes in the paragraphs written above by means outlined in the second paragraph of Article 311 will be increased accordingly.*

Anti-Terror Law/Terörle Mücadele Kanunu (No. 3713, Adopted April 12, 1991)

Article 8—Propaganda against the indivisibility of the State—(Amended: 1995\4126.1)

> *Written or oral propaganda, along with meetings, demonstrations, and marches, that have the goal of destroying the indivisible unity of the state with its territory and nation of the Republic of Turkey cannot be conducted. Those who conduct such activities shall be punished with imprisonment of between one and three years and a heavy fine of between 100 million lira and 300 million lira. If this crime is conducted habitually, imprisonment cannot be converted into a monetary fine....*[331]

---

[329]Fine later increased three times.

[330]Fine later increased three times.

[331]Parliament amended the Anti-Terror Law in October 1995. Before its amendment, Article 8 punished all so-called separatist propaganda "regardless of the method, intent, or idea behind it."

If the propaganda crime determined in the first paragraph is committed by means of periodicals determined in the third article of the Press Law No. 5860, the owner will also be given a monetary fine of an amount up to ninety percent of the past month's average sales even if the frequency of the periodical is less than a month. This fine, however, cannot be less than 100 million lira. The responsible editor of the periodicals will be subject to one-half of the monetary fine given to the owner as well as imprisonment of between six months and two years.

If the propaganda crime determined in the first paragraph is committed by press works or other mass communication instruments outside of the written periodicals in the second paragraph, the responsible editor as well as the owners of the means of mass communication will face imprisonment of between six months and two years and a heavy fine of between 100-300 million lira. In addition, if the act is committed by means of radio or television, a broadcast prohibition of between one and fifteen days can be given to the said radio and television stations.

If carried out by means explained in the second paragraph or by methods of mass communication outlined in the third paragraph, the punishment determined in paragraph one will increase from one-third to one-half.

Political Parties Law/ Siyasi Partiler Kanunu (No. 2820, Adopted April 26, 1982)

Article 81: Preventing the Creation of Minorities

Political parties:

a) cannot put forward that minorities exist in the Turkish Republic based on national, religious, confessional, racial, or language differences....

b) cannot by means of protecting, developing, or disseminating language or cultures other than the Turkish language and culture through creating minorities in the Republic of Turkey have the goal of destroying national unity or be engaged in activities to this end;

c) cannot use a language other than Turkish in writing and printing party statute or program, at congresses, at meetings in open air or indoor gatherings; at meetings, and in propaganda, cannot use or distribute placards, pictures, phonograph records, voice and visual tapes, brochures and statements written in a language other than Turkish; cannot remain indifferent to these actions and acts committed by others; however, it is possible to translate party statutes and programs into foreign languages other than those forbidden by law.

The Law concerning the Founding and Broadcasts of Television and Radio/ Radyo ve Televizyonları n Kuruluş ve Yayınları Hakkında Kanun (No. 3984, Adopted April 13, 1994)[332]

Article 4: Broadcasting principles:

Radio and Television broadcast are to be carried out in the understanding of public service according to the principles below:

Broadcasts cannot be contradictory to the following:

a) the existence and independence of the Turkish Republic, the indivisible unity of the state with its territory and nation;

b) the national and spiritual values of society....

d) the general morality, civil peace, and structure of the Turkish family;

Must be conducted in accordance with:

h) the general goals and basic principles of Turkish national education and the development of national culture;

i) fairness and objectivity in broadcasting and the fundamental principle of respect for the law....

---

[332]Until 1993, television and radio broadcasting was state controlled under Article 133 of the constitution. In 1993, parliament amended Article 133 to allow for private radio and television stations.

l) to present news in a speedy and correct way;

m) the principle that broadcasts will not be made that have a negative effect on the physical, intellectual, mental, and moral development of children and youth....

t) radio and television broadcasts will be made in Turkish; however, for the purpose of teaching or of imparting news those foreign languages that have made a contribution to the development of universal cultural and scientific works can be used.

Foreign Language Education and Teaching Law (No. 2923)

Article 2

a) The mother tongue of Turkish citizens cannot be taught in any language other than Turkish....

c) Taking into consideration the view of the National Security Council, the Council of Ministers by its decision will determine in Turkey what foreign languages can be taught.

Decision No. 92/2788, *Official Gazette*, March 20, 1992

2—...It had been decided by the Council of Ministers on March 4, 1992 that in official and private courses education and teaching are to be made in the following languages: English, French, German as well as Russian, Italian, Spanish, Arabic, Japanese, and Chinese.

The law concerning fundamental provisions on elections and voter registries/ Seçimlerin Temel Hükümleri ve Seçmen Kütükleri Hakkında Kanun (No. 298, Adopted April 26, 1961)

Article 58

....It is forbidden to use any other language or script than Turkish in propaganda disseminated in radio or television as well as in other election propaganda.

Press Law/ Basın Kanunu (No. 5680, Adopted July 15, 1950)

Article 1

>*The press is free.*

>*The publishing of printed works is subject to the written directives in this*
law.

Article 16—Criminal responsibility for crimes committed by means of the press--
(Amended 1983/2950)

>*1. The responsibility for crimes committed in periodicals belongs,*
together with the person who caused the crime, whether the writer, news
writer, artist, or caricaturist, to the periodical's responsible editor.
However, punishment's depriving liberty given to responsible editors
without regard to their duration shall be converted to monetary fines....
Responsible editors cannot be punished with security detention.

>*2. The responsible editor is not required to give the name of writers, news*
writers, artists, or caricaturists who publish with a pen name or alias.
Without regard to the first paragraph, the responsibility for a writing, or
a news report, or a picture, or a caricature, where the author of a work
is not clear or where the author's names is not revealed in a true manner
by the responsible editor at the latest during the first court interrogation,
shall fall to the responsible editor as if he were the person who through
writing, or news writing, or making a picture or caricature caused the
crime.

>*3. The responsible editor is not responsible for writings, news, pictures,*
or caricatures published by the periodical's owner without his approval.
Under such circumstances, the legal responsibility of the responsible
editor belongs to the person who publishes the writing, news, picture, or
caricature.

>*4. In crimes that are committed in publications that are not defined as*
periodicals [books], the legal responsibility belongs to the publisher
together with the writer, translator, or artist. However, regardless of the
duration, all verdicts giving the penalty of imprisonment for the publisher

shall be converted to fines. Computation of the fine is based on the amount mentioned in the Law No. 647 on the Execution of Penalties, Article 4, Paragraph 1. Publishers are not to be penalized with security detention.

In the case where the author of the printed work published as a non-periodical is not identified, the responsibility belongs to the publisher without regard to the aforementioned articles. In the case when the work is published without the knowledge and consent of its writer, translator, or artist, only the publisher becomes responsible as if the one who created the work.

When the above mentioned persons are not identified or a case in a Turkish court is not opened against them, the responsibility belongs to the seller and distributor when the publisher is not known.

In quotations that are made in publications published in Turkey without the consent of the owner, the responsibility belongs to the one who made the quote.

If publication is made in any language prohibited by law, the relevant articles which envision converting into monetary fines and of not giving a penalty of placing under security detention shall not be applied.

Article 31—(Amended 1983/2950)

The entry or distribution into Turkey of works published in a foreign country that contradict the indivisible unity of the state with its territory and nation, national hegemony, the existence of the Republic, national security, public order, general law and order, the common good, general morality or health can be outlawed by a decision of the Council of Ministers.

Provincial Administration Law/ İl İdaresi Kanunu (No. 5442, Adopted June 10, 1949)

Article 2/d/2 (Amended 1959:7267)

Village names that are not Turkish and give rise to confusion are to be changed in the shortest possible time by the Interior Ministry after receiving the opinion of the Provincial Permanent Committee.

Police Duty and Responsibility Law/ Polis Vazife ve Selâhiyet Kanunu (No. 2559, Adopted July 4, 1934)

Article 8—(Amended: 1985/3233)

If the police are in possession of incontrovertible evidence and by order of the district's highest civil servant, areas where plays are conducted, presentations given, films or videos shown that will damage the indivisible unity of the state with its territory and nation, constitutional order, or general security or common morality can be closed by the police or have their activities stopped.

If the reason for the closing or ceasing of activities require a legal investigation by the state, the investigation file shall be immediately given to the judiciary....

The Law concerning crimes committed against Atatürk/ Atatürk Aleyhine İşlenen Suçlar Hakkında Kanun (No. 5816, Adopted July 25, 1951)

Article 1

Anyone who publicly insults or curses the memory of Atatürk shall be imprisoned with a heavy sentence of between one and three years.

A heavy sentence of between one and five years shall be given to anyone who destroys, breaks, ruins, or defaces a statue, bust, or monuments representing Atatürk or the grave of Atatürk.

Anyone who encourages others to commit the crimes outlined in the paragraphs above will be punished as if committing the crime.

Article 2

> *If the crimes outlined in the first article are committed by a group of two or more individuals, or publicly, or in public districts or by means of the press will have the penalty imposed increased by a proportion of one-half.*
>
> *If the crimes outlined in the second paragraph of the first article are committed using force...the penalty will be doubled... .*